W9-AJC-745

LET'S LEARN

絵とき辞書で日本語を学びましょう

JAPANESE

PICTURE DICTIONARY

By
The Editors of
Passport Books

Illustrated by
Marlene Goodman

PASSPORT BOOKS
NTC/Contemporary Publishing Company

Welcome to the *Let's Learn Japanese* Picture Dictionary!

Here's an exciting way for you to learn more than 1,500 words that will help you speak about many of your favorite subjects. With these words, you will be able to talk about your house, sports, outer space, the ocean, and many more subjects.

This dictionary is fun to use. On each page, you will see drawings with the words that describe them underneath. These drawings are usually part of a large, colorful scene. See if you can find all the words in the big scene! You will enjoy looking at the pictures more and more as you learn new words.

At the back of the book, you will find a Japanese-English Glossary and Index and an English-Japanese Glossary and Index, where you can look up words in alphabetical order, and find out exactly where the words are located in the dictionary.

This is a book you can look at over and over again, and each time you look, you will find something new. You'll be able to talk about people, places, and things you know, and you'll learn lots of new words as you go along!

Library of Congress Cataloging-in-Publication Data
is available from the United States Library of Congress.

Illustrations by Terrie Meider
7. Clothing; 15. People in our Community; 18. Sports; 28. Colors;
29. The Family Tree; 30. Shapes; 31. Numbers; 32. Map of the World.

Published by Passport Books
An imprint of NTC/Contemporary Publishing Company
4255 West Touhy Avenue, Lincolnwood (Chicago), Illinois 60646-1975 U.S.A.
Copyright © 1992 by NTC/Contemporary Publishing Company
Printed in Hong Kong
International Standard Book Number: 0-8442-8494-7

8 9 WKT 12 11 10

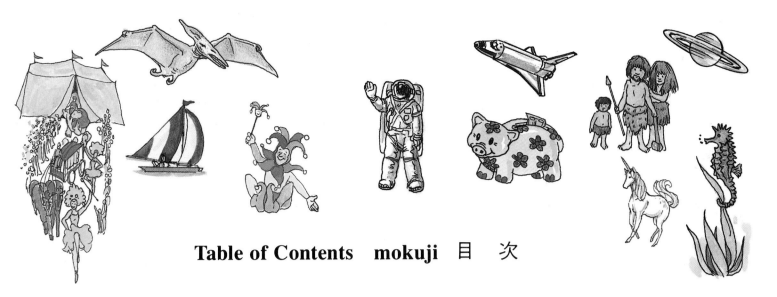

Table of Contents   mokuji   目 次

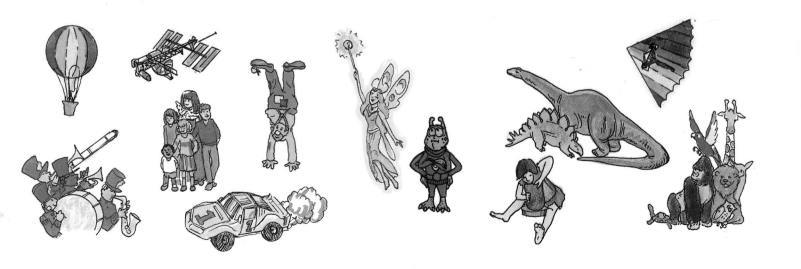

1. Our Classroom kyōshitsu 教室

teacher (male)
sensei (otoko)
先生（男）

teacher (female)
sensei (onna)
先生（女）

student (male)
gakusei, seito (otoko)
学生，生徒（男）

student (female)
gakusei, seito (onna)
学生，生徒（女）

map
chizu
地図

chalkboard
kokuban
黒板

chalk
chōku
チョーク

(chalkboard) eraser
kokubanfuki
黒板ふき

trash
kuzu
くず

wastebasket
kuzukago
くずかご

stapler
hotchikisu
ホッチキス

staples
hotchikisu no hari
ホッチキスの針

teacher's desk
sensei no tsukue
先生の机

calendar
karendā
カレンダー

cellophane tape
serotēpu
セロテープ

notebook
nōto
ノート

bookcase
honbako
本箱

bulletin board
keijiban
掲示板

arithmetic problem
sansū no mondai
算数の問題

calculator
keisanki
計算器

alphabet
arufabetto
アルファベット

ABCD

easel
gaka
画架

protractor
bundoki
分度器

pen
pen, borupen
ペン，ボールペン

colored pencils
iroenpitsu
色鉛筆

pupil desk
seito no tsukue
生徒の机

aquarium
suisō
水槽

fish
sakana
魚

loudspeaker
supiikā
スピーカー

book
hon
本

rug
shikimono
敷き物

ruler
jōgi
定規

scissors
hasami
はさみ

bell
kane
鐘

hole punch
ana akeki
穴あけ器

compass
konpasu
コンパス

(pencil) eraser
keshigomu
消しゴム

pencil
enpitsu
鉛筆

pencil sharpener
enpitsu kezuri
鉛筆削り

clock
tokei
時計

numbers
sū
数

cactus
saboten
さぼてん

hand
(tokei no) hari
（時計の）針

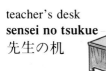

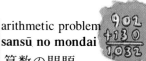

plant
shokubutsu
植物

glue
setchakuzai
接着剤

globe
chikyūgi
地球儀

picture
e
絵

paint
enogu
絵の具

paintbrush
efude
絵筆

paper
kami
紙

crayon
kureyon
クレヨン

2. Our House   ie, jūtaku   家，住宅

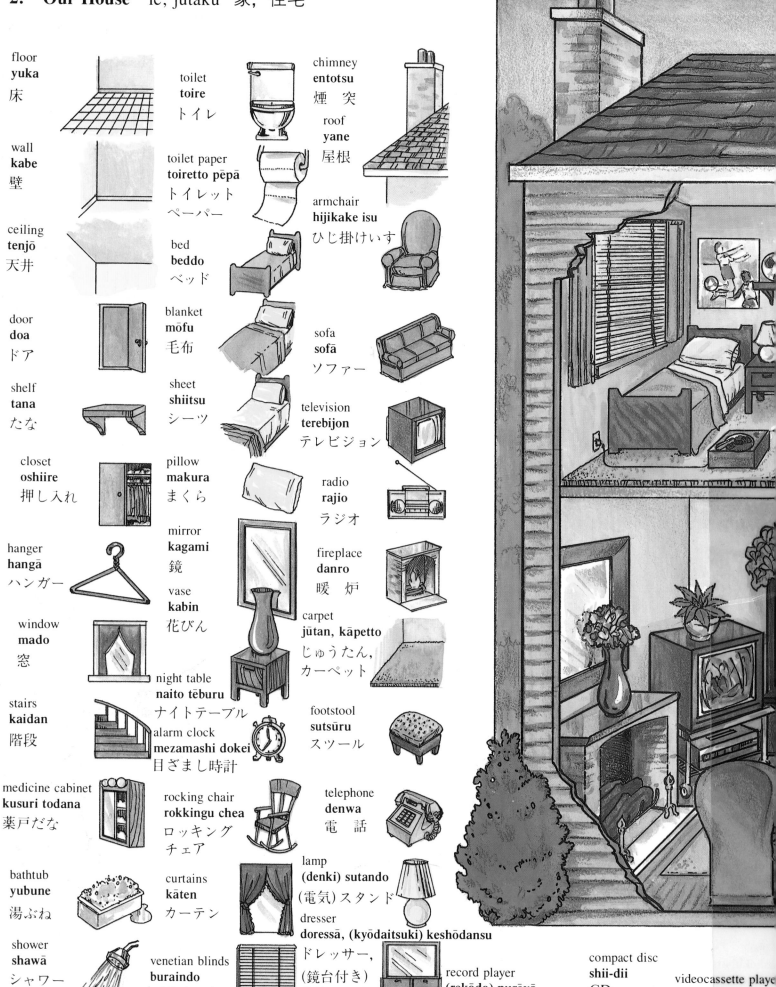

floor
yuka
床

wall
kabe
壁

ceiling
tenjō
天井

door
doa
ドア

shelf
tana
たな

closet
oshiire
押し入れ

hanger
hangā
ハンガー

window
mado
窓

stairs
kaidan
階段

medicine cabinet
kusuri todana
薬戸だな

bathtub
yubune
湯ぶね

shower
shawā
シャワー

towel
taoru
タオル

toilet
toire
トイレ

toilet paper
toiretto pēpā
トイレット
ペーパー

bed
beddo
ベッド

blanket
mōfu
毛布

sheet
shiitsu
シーツ

pillow
makura
まくら

mirror
kagami
鏡

vase
kabin
花びん

night table
naito tēburu
ナイトテーブル

alarm clock
mezamashi dokei
目ざまし時計

rocking chair
rokkingu chea
ロッキング
チェア

curtains
kāten
カーテン

venetian blinds
buraindo
ブラインド

poster
posutā
ポスター

chimney
entotsu
煙突

roof
yane
屋根

armchair
hijikake isu
ひじ掛けいす

sofa
sofā
ソファー

television
terebijon
テレビジョン

radio
rajio
ラジオ

fireplace
danro
暖炉

carpet
jūtan, kāpetto
じゅうたん，
カーペット

footstool
sutsūru
スツール

telephone
denwa
電話

lamp
(denki) sutando
（電気）スタンド

dresser
doressā, (kyōdaitsuki) keshōdansu
ドレッサー，
（鏡台付き）
化粧だんす

record player
(rekōdo) purēyā
（レコード）プレーヤー

record
rekōdo
レコード

compact disc
shii-dii
CD

videocassette player
bideo dekki
ビデオデッキ

| | | bedroom
shinshitsu
寝　室 | bathroom
yokushitsu
浴　室 | living room
ima
居　間 | dining room
dainingu rūmu
ダイニングルーム | kitchen
daidokoro
台　所 |

cassette tape
kasetto tēpu
セットテープ

cassette player
kasetto dekki
カセットデッキ

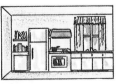

3. The Kitchen daidokoro 台所

counter
kauntā
カウンタ

table
tēburu
テーブル

microwave oven
denshi renji
電子レンジ

stove
konro, renji
こんろ, レンジ
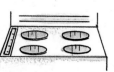

oven
ōbun, tenpi
オーブン, 天火

refrigerator
reizōko
冷蔵庫

freezer
furiizā
フリーザー

sink
(daidokoro no) nagashi
(台所の)流し

faucet
jaguchi, kokku
じゃ口, コック

dishwasher
(jidō) sara araiki
(自動)皿洗い機

food processor
fūdo purosessā (bannō chōri yōgu)
フードプロセッサー
(万能調理用具)

kettle
yakan
やかん

pan
furaipan
フライパン

electric mixer
mikisā
ミキサー

drawer
hikidashi
引き出し

toaster
tōsutā
トースター

paper towels
pēpā taoru
ペーパータオル

ice cubes
kakugōri
角氷

spatula
furaigaeshi
フライ返し

dishes
sara
皿

chair
isu
いす

apron
epuron
エプロン

flour
komugiko
小麦粉

sponge
suponji
スポンジ

washing machine
sentakuki
洗たく機

iron
airon
アイロン

screw
neji
ねじ

toolbox
dōgubako
道具箱

laundry detergent
senzai
洗　剤

laundry
sentakumono
洗たく物

broom
hōki
ほうき

mop
moppu
モップ

screwdriver
nejimawashi
ねじ回し

wrench
supanā, renchi
スパナー, レンチ

wood
mokuzai
木材

board
ita
板

vacuum cleaner
denki sōjiki
電気そうじ機

dustpan
chiritori
ちり取り

drill
doriru
ドリル

electrical outlet
konsento
コンセント

sandpaper
kamiyasuri
紙やすり

flashlight
kaichū dentō
懐中電燈

ironing board
airondai
アイロン台

hammer
kanazuchi
金づち

brick
renga
れんが

clothes dryer
(sentakumono no) kansōki
(洗たく物の)乾燥器

nail
kugi
くぎ

file
yasuri
やすり

tape measure
makijaku
巻き尺

saw
nokogiri
のこぎり

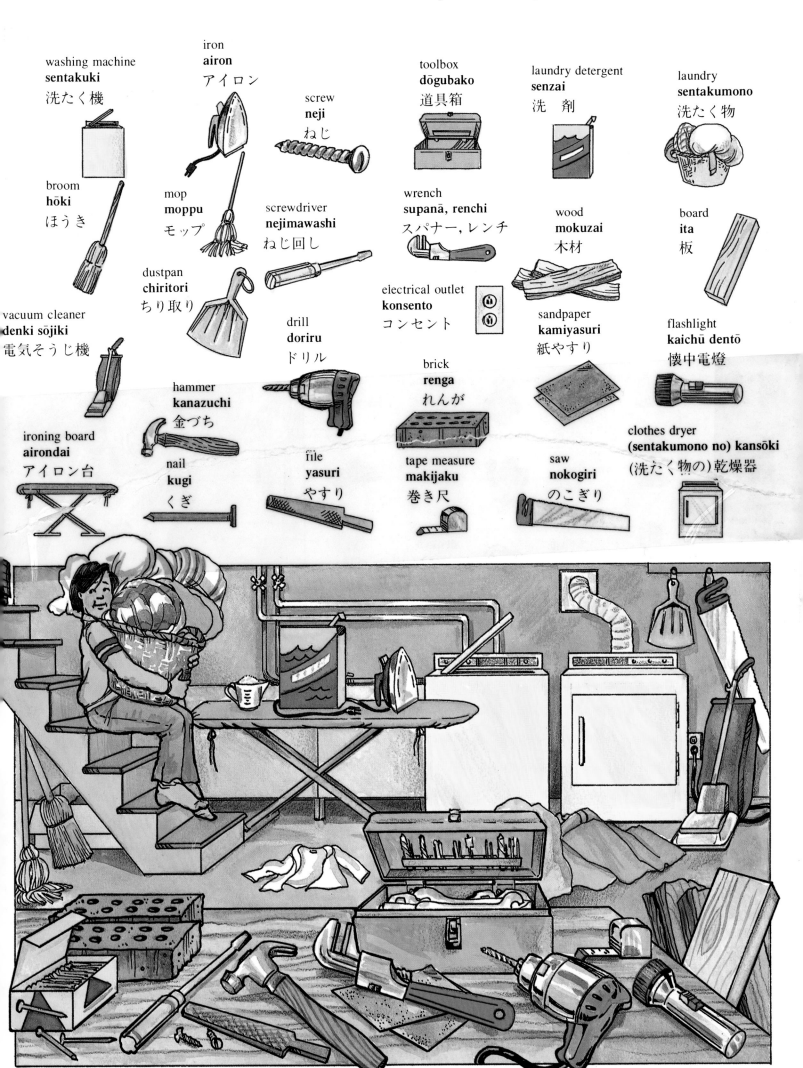

4. The Attic   yaneura beya   屋根裏部屋

trunk
toranku
トランク

box
hako
箱

dust
hokori, chiri
ほこり, ちり
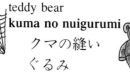

string
himo, ito
ひも, 糸

cobweb
kumo no su
くもの巣

ball gown
butōkaiyō doresu
舞踏会用ドレス
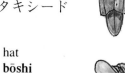

top hat
shiruku hatto
シルクハット

tuxedo
takishiido
タキシード

hat
bōshi
帽子
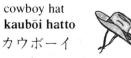

feather
hane
羽

cowboy hat
kaubōi hatto
カウボーイ
ハット
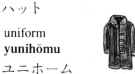

uniform
yunihōmu
ユニホーム

cowboy boots
kaubōi būtsu
カウボーイブーツ

photo album
arubamu
アルバム

game
gēmu, gēmuban
ゲーム,
ゲーム盤

doll
ningyō
人形

jigsaw puzzle
jigusō pazuru
ジグソーパズル

jump rope
tobinawa
飛びなわ

teddy bear
kuma no nuigurumi
クマの縫い
ぐるみ

toys
omocha
おもちゃ

whistle
fue
笛

cards
toranpu
トランプ

dice
saikoro
さいころ

blocks
tsumiki
積み木

electric train
denki kikansha
電気機関車

magnet
jishaku
磁石

cradle
yurikago
揺りかご

coloring book
nurie
ぬりえ

music box
orugōru
オルゴール

yarn
keito
毛糸

knitting needles
amibari
編み針

dollhouse
ningyō no ie
人形の家

comic books
mangabon
漫画本

lightbulb
denkyū
電球

toy soldiers
omocha no heitai
おもちゃの兵隊

movie projector
eishaki
映写機

umbrella
kasa
かさ

puppet
yubi ningyō
ゆび人形

fan
sensu
扇子

marbles
ohajiki
おはじき

rocking horse
yuri mokuba
揺り木馬

chess
chesu
チェス

photograph
shashin
写 真

spinning wheel
itoguruma, tsumugiguruma
糸車, 紡ぎ車

picture frame
gakubuchi
額 縁

rocking chair
rokkingu chea
ロッキングチェア

checkers
chekkā
チェッカー

5. The Four Seasons (Weather)   shiki (tenkō)   四季(天候)

Winter   fuyu   冬

snow **yuki** 雪		sled **sori** そり
ice **kōri** 氷		snowplow **josetsusha (ki)** 除雪車(機)
snowflake **setsuhen** 雪片		snowmobile **setsujōsha** 雪上車
icicle **tsurara** つらら		snowman **yukidaruma** 雪だるま
shovel **shaberu** シャベル		snowball **yuki no tama** 雪の玉
snowstorm **fubuki** 吹雪		log **maruta** 丸太

Spring   haru   春

rain **ame** 雨	flowers **hana** 花
rainbow **niji** にじ	flowerbed **kadan** 花壇
stem **kuki** 茎	petal **hanabira** 花びら
bird **tori** 鳥	vegetable garden **katei saien** 家庭菜園
worm **mushi** 虫	
raindrop **amadare** 雨だれ	lightning **inazuma** いなずま

Summer natsu 夏

butterfly
chō
ちょう

fly
hae
はえ

fly swatter
haetataki
はえたたき

fan
senpūki
扇風機

sprinkler
supurinkurā
スプリンクラー

grasshopper
batta, kirigirisu
バッタ, キリギリス

lawn mower
shibakariki
芝刈り機

barbecue
bābekyū
バーベキュー

hammock
hanmokku
ハンモック

yard
niwa
庭

deck
barukonii, rodai
バルコニー,
露台

garden hose
mizumaki hōsu
水まきホース

matches
matchi
マッチ

Fall aki 秋

wind
kaze
風

leaf
ha
葉

branch
eda
枝

fog
kiri
霧

rake
kumade
くまで

clouds
kumo
雲

kite
tako
たこ

puddle
mizutamari
水たまり

mud
doro
どろ

bird's nest
tori no su
鳥の巣

bush
kanboku
かん木

6. At the Supermarket sūpāmāketto スーパーマーケット

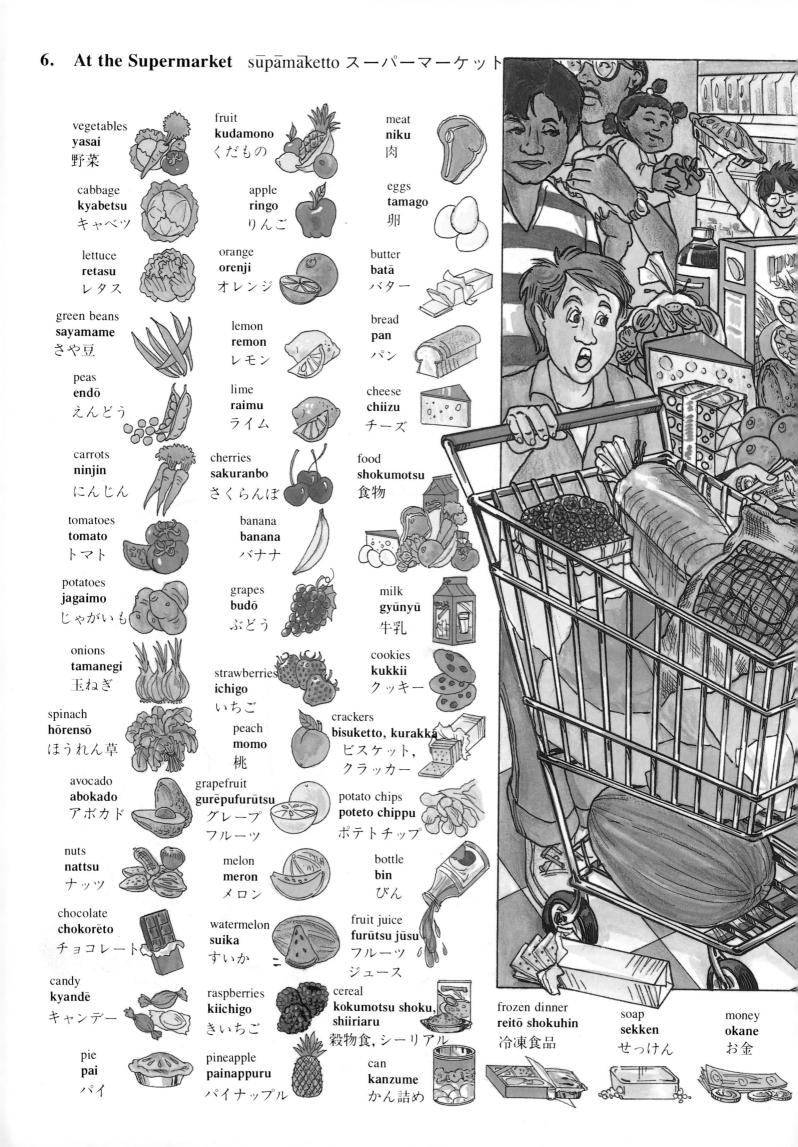

vegetables
yasai
野菜

cabbage
kyabetsu
キャベツ

lettuce
retasu
レタス

green beans
sayamame
さや豆

peas
endō
えんどう

carrots
ninjin
にんじん

tomatoes
tomato
トマト

potatoes
jagaimo
じゃがいも

onions
tamanegi
玉ねぎ

spinach
hōrensō
ほうれん草

avocado
abokado
アボカド

nuts
nattsu
ナッツ

chocolate
chokorēto
チョコレート

candy
kyandē
キャンデー

pie
pai
パイ

fruit
kudamono
くだもの

apple
ringo
りんご

orange
orenji
オレンジ

lemon
remon
レモン

lime
raimu
ライム

cherries
sakuranbo
さくらんぼ

banana
banana
バナナ

grapes
budō
ぶどう

strawberries
ichigo
いちご

peach
momo
桃

grapefruit
gurēpufurūtsu
グレープ
フルーツ

melon
meron
メロン

watermelon
suika
すいか

raspberries
kiichigo
きいちご

pineapple
painappuru
パイナップル

meat
niku
肉

eggs
tamago
卵

butter
batā
バター

bread
pan
パン

cheese
chiizu
チーズ

food
shokumotsu
食物

milk
gyūnyū
牛乳

cookies
kukkii
クッキー

crackers
bisuketto, kurakkā
ビスケット,
クラッカー

potato chips
poteto chippu
ポテトチップ

bottle
bin
びん

fruit juice
furūtsu jūsu
フルーツ
ジュース

cereal
kokumotsu shoku,
shiiriaru
穀物食, シーリアル

can
kanzume
かん詰め

frozen dinner
reitō shokuhin
冷凍食品

soap
sekken
せっけん

money
okane
お金

shopping cart
kaimono guruma
買い物車

shopping bag
kaimono bukuro
買い物袋

sign
hyōshiki, hyōji
標識,
表示

scale
hakari
はかり

price
nedan
値段

cash register
rejisutā
レジスター

cashier
rejisutā gakari
レジスター係

7. Clothing mi ni tsukeru mono 身につけるもの

glasses
megane
めがね

buckle
shimegane
締め金

belt
beruto
ベルト

collar
karā, eri
カラー, えり

blouse
burausu
ブラウス

bracelet
buresuretto
ブレスレット

ring
yubiwa
指輪

skirt
sukāto
スカート

socks
sokkusu
ソックス

shoes
kutsu
くつ

pants
zubon
ズボン

underwear
shitagi
下着

tie
nekutai
ネクタイ

necklace
nekkuresu
ネックレス

sleeve
sode
そで

dress
fuku, doresu
服, ドレス

earmuffs
mimiate
耳あて

button
botan
ボタン

bathing suit
mizugi
水着

shirt
shatsu
シャツ

suit
sebiro, sūtsu
背広, スーツ

gloves
tebukuro
手袋

shoelace
kutsuhimo
くつひも

handkerchief
hankachi
ハンカチ

coat
uwagi
上着

sweater
sētā
セーター

gym shoes
undōgutsu
運動ぐつ

tights
taitsu
タイツ

hat
bōshi
帽子

sunglasses
sangurasu
サングラス

earring
iyaringu
イヤリング

shorts
hanzubon
半ズボン

sandals
sandaru
サンダル

backpack
ryukkusakku
リュックサック

down vest
chokki, besuto
チョッキ，ベスト

jeans
jiipan
ジーパン

hiking boots
haikinguyō kutsu
ハイキング用くつ

sweatshirt
torēningu shatsu
トレーニングシャツ

sweatpants
torēningu pantsu
トレーニングパンツ

t-shirt
t-shatsu
Tシャツ

watch
udedokei
腕時計

scarf
erimaki
えり巻き

jacket
uwagi
上着

mittens
miton
ミトン

umbrella
kasa
かさ

hood
fūdo
フード

raincoat
rēnkōto
レーンコート

pocket
poketto
ポケット

zipper
chakku, jippā
チャック，ジッパー

boots
būtsu
ブーツ

bathrobe
basurōbu
バスローブ

pajamas
pajama
パジャマ

cap
kyappu
キャップ

8. In the City toshi 都市

building
tatemono, biru
建物，ビル

apartment building
apāto
アパート

train station
(tetsudō no) eki
（鉄道の）駅

skyscraper
chōkōsō biru
超高層ビル

fire escape
hijō kaidan
非常階段

church
kyōkai
教会

factory
kōba
工場

balcony
barukonii
バルコニー

school
gakkō
学校

smokestack
entotsu
煙突

fire station
shōbōsho
消防署

museum
hakubutsukan
博物館

traffic light
kōtsū shingōki
交通信号燈

police station
keisatsusho
警察署

hospital
byōin
病院

manhole cover
manhōru no futa
マンホールのふた

jail
keimusho
刑務所

drugstore
(pharmacy)
yakkyoku
薬局

driveway
shadō
車道

bookstore
hon'ya
本屋

parking lot
chūshajō
駐車場

toy store
omochaya
おもちゃ屋

movie theater
eigakan
映画館

parking meter
pākingu mētā
パーキング
メーター

grocery story
yaoya
八百屋

restaurant
resutoran
レストラン

corner
**magarikado,
kado, machikado**
曲がりかど，
かど，町かど

bakery
pan'ya
パン屋

clothing store
yōfukuya
洋服屋

fire hydrant
shōkasen
消火せん

butcher shop
nikuya
肉屋

hotel
hoteru
ホテル

square
hiroba
広場

fountain
funsui
噴水

traffic jam
kōtsū jūtai
交通渋滞

statue
zō
像

newspaper
shinbun
新聞

crane
kurēn
クレーン

bench
benchi
ベンチ

sign
hyōshiki, kanban
標識，看板

playground
asobiba
遊び場

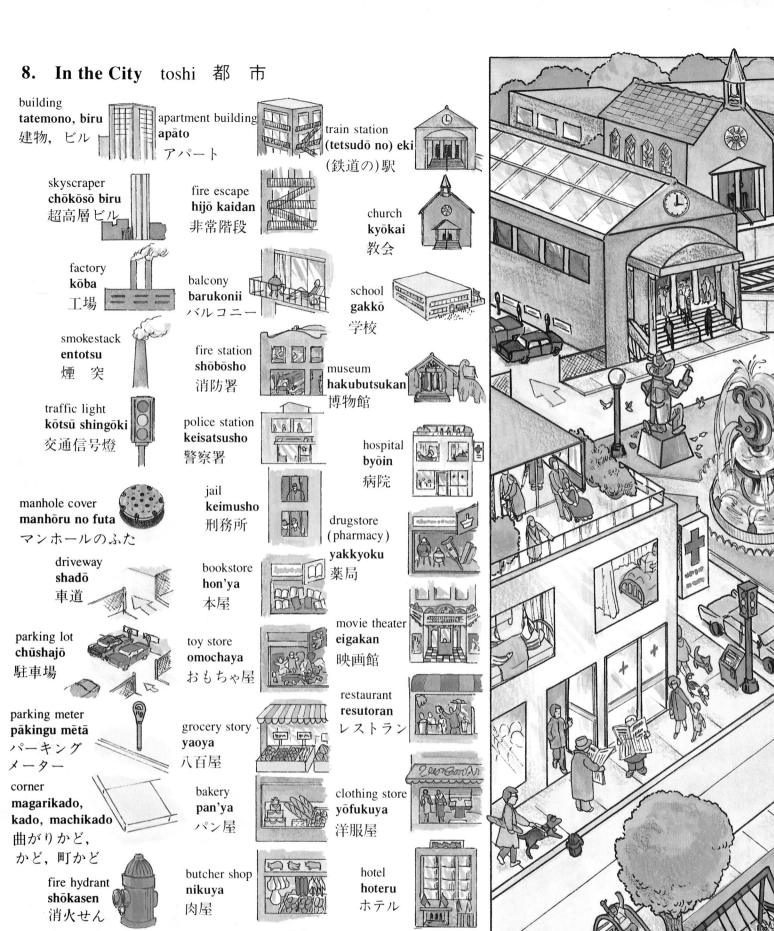

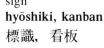

park **kōen** 公園	jungle gym **janguru jimu** ジャングルジム	swings **buranko** ぶらんこ	seesaw **shiisō** シーソー	slide **suberidai** すべり台	sandbox **sunaba** 砂場	beach **hama** 浜

9. In the Country inaka 田舎

farmer
nōfu
農夫

tractor
torakutā
トラクター

barn
naya,
kachiku
goya
納屋，家
畜小屋

hay
hoshikusa
干し草

dog
inu
犬

puppy
koinu
子犬

cat
neko
ねこ

kitten
koneko
子ねこ

rooster
ondori
おんどり

hen
mendori
めんどり

chick
hiyoko
ひよこ

pig
buta
ぶた

piglet
kobuta
子ぶた

rabbit
usagi
うさぎ

bull
oushi
雄牛

cow
meushi
雌牛

calf
koushi
子牛

horse
uma
馬

colt
kouma
子馬

duck
ahiru
あひる

duckling
ahiru no ko
あひるの子

goat
yagi
やぎ

kid
koyagi
子やぎ

goose
gachō
がちょう

gosling
gachō no hina
がちょうのひな

sheep
hitsuji
羊

lamb
kohitsuji
子羊

mouse
nezumi
ねずみ

horns
tsuno
角

donkey
roba
ろば

bees
mitsubachi
みつばち

frog
kaeru
かえる

pond
ike
池

grass
kusa
草

fence
kakoi
囲い

tree
ki
木

shadow
kage
影

hill
oka
丘

road
dōro
道路

smoke
kemuri
煙

picnic
pikunikku
ピクニック

ant
ari
あり

dirt
gomi
ごみ

tent
tento
テント

sky
sora
空

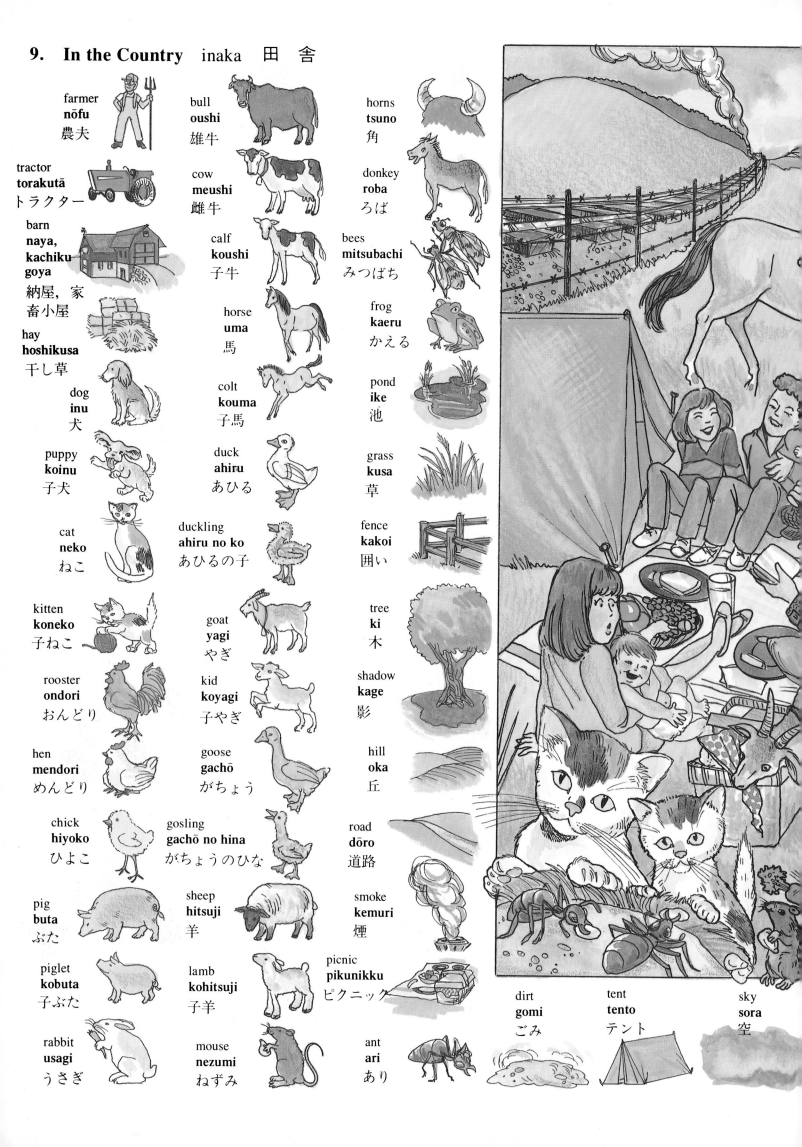

train tracks
senro
線路

sleeping bag
nebukuro
寝袋

man
otoko
男

woman
onna
女

boy
shōnen
少年

girl
shōjo
少女

baby
akanbō
赤ん坊

farm
nōjō
農場

10. In a Restaurant resutoran レストラン

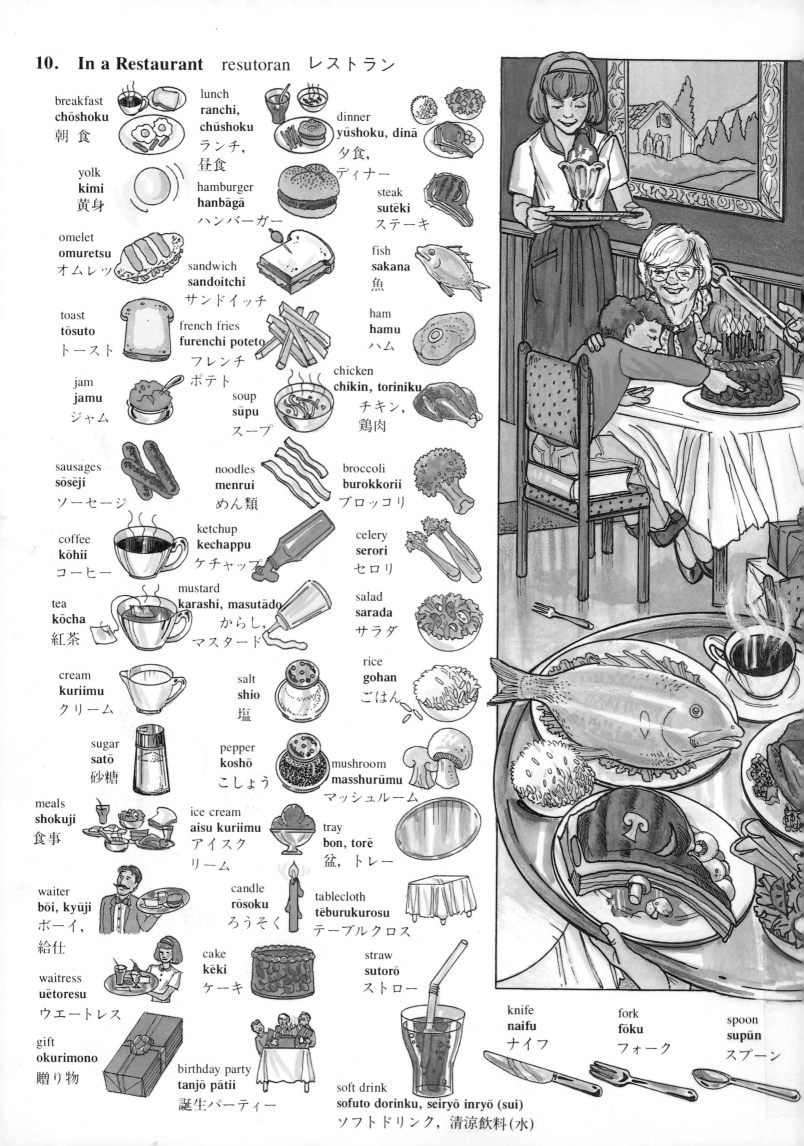

breakfast
chōshoku
朝食

yolk
kimi
黄身

omelet
omuretsu
オムレツ

toast
tōsuto
トースト

jam
jamu
ジャム

sausages
sōsēji
ソーセージ

coffee
kōhii
コーヒー

tea
kōcha
紅茶

cream
kuriimu
クリーム

sugar
satō
砂糖

meals
shokuji
食事

waiter
bōi, kyūji
ボーイ,
給仕

waitress
uētoresu
ウエートレス

gift
okurimono
贈り物

lunch
ranchi,
chūshoku
ランチ,
昼食

hamburger
hanbāgā
ハンバーガー

sandwich
sandoitchi
サンドイッチ

french fries
furenchi poteto
フレンチ
ポテト

soup
sūpu
スープ

noodles
menrui
めん類

ketchup
kechappu
ケチャップ

mustard
karashi, masutādo
からし,
マスタード

salt
shio
塩

pepper
koshō
こしょう

ice cream
aisu kuriimu
アイスク
リーム

candle
rōsoku
ろうそく

cake
kēki
ケーキ

birthday party
tanjō pātii
誕生パーティー

dinner
yūshoku, dinā
夕食,
ディナー

steak
sutēki
ステーキ

fish
sakana
魚

ham
hamu
ハム

chicken
chikin, toriniku
チキン,
鶏肉

broccoli
burokkorii
ブロッコリ

celery
serori
セロリ

salad
sarada
サラダ

rice
gohan
ごはん

mushroom
masshurūmu
マッシュルーム

tray
bon, torē
盆, トレー

tablecloth
tēburukurosu
テーブルクロス

straw
sutorō
ストロー

soft drink
sofuto dorinku, seiryō inryō (sui)
ソフトドリンク, 清涼飲料(水)

knife
naifu
ナイフ

fork
fōku
フォーク

spoon
supūn
スプーン

| plate
sara
皿 | saucer
ukezare
受け皿 | cup
kappu, chawan
カップ, 茶わん | glass
koppu, gurasu
コップ, グラス | | napkin
napukin
ナプキン | menu
menyū
メニュー  |

bowl
bōru, donburi　ボール,　どんぶり

11. The Doctor's Office iin 医院

doctor
isha
医者

cast
gipusu
ギプス

examining table
shinsatsudai
診察台

wheelchair
kuruma isu
車いす

nurse
kangofu
看護婦

sling
tsuri hōtai
つり包帯

sneeze
kushami
くしゃみ

foot
ashi
足

patient
kanja
患者

hypodermic needle
chūsha bari
注射針

arm
ude
腕

ankle
ashikubi
足首

medicine
naifukuyaku
内服薬

blood
chi
血

elbow
hiji
ひじ

toe
ashi no yubi
足の指

pill
jōzai
錠剤

cane
tsue
つえ

hand
te
手

shoulder
kata
肩

thermometer
taionkei
温度計

finger
yubi
指

back
se
背

crutch
matsubazue
松葉づえ

thumb
oyayubi
親指

chest
mune
胸

bandage
hōtai
包帯

stethoscope
chōshinki
聴診器

leg
ashi
足

knee
hiza
ひざ

The Dentist's Office   shikaiin 歯科医院

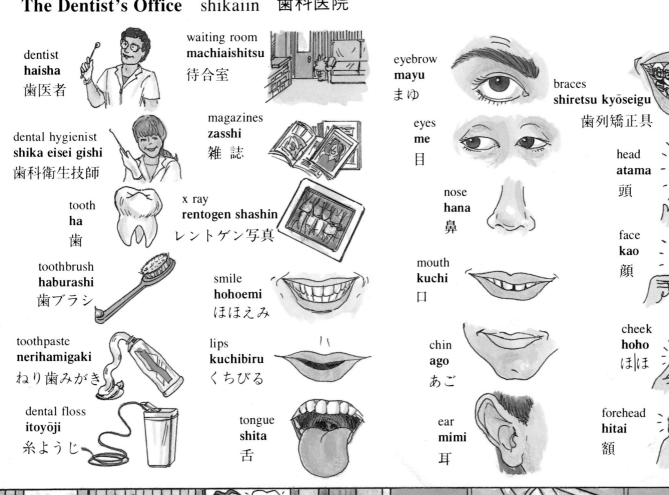

dentist
haisha
歯医者

waiting room
machiaishitsu
待合室

dental hygienist
shika eisei gishi
歯科衛生技師

magazines
zasshi
雑誌

tooth
ha
歯

x ray
rentogen shashin
レントゲン写真

toothbrush
haburashi
歯ブラシ

smile
hohoemi
ほほえみ

toothpaste
nerihamigaki
ねり歯みがき

lips
kuchibiru
くちびる

dental floss
itoyōji
糸ようじ

tongue
shita
舌

eyebrow
mayu
まゆ

eyes
me
目

nose
hana
鼻

mouth
kuchi
口

chin
ago
あご

ear
mimi
耳

braces
shiretsu kyōseigu
歯列矯正具

head
atama
頭

face
kao
顔

cheek
hoho
ほほ

forehead
hitai
額

hairstylist
hea dezainā
ヘアデザイナー

mousse
(hea) mūsu
（ヘア）ムース

barrette
hea pin
ヘアピン

shampoo
shanpū
シャンプー

manicurist
manikyuashi
マニキュア師

braid
osagegame
おさげ髪

suds
sekken no awa
せっけんの
あわ

fingernail
yubi no tsume
指のつめ

wavy
uēbu no kakatta
ウエーブの
かかった

comb
kushi
くし

nail polish
nēru enameru
ネールエナメル

straight
**(chijirete inai)
massugu na**
（縮れていない
まっすぐな

brush
burashi
ブラシ

lipstick
kuchibeni
口紅

curly
kāru shita
カールした

scissors
hasami
はさみ

mascara
masukara
マスカラ

short
mijikai
短い

curlers
kārā
カーラー

powder
oshiroi
おしろい

long
nagai
長い

curling iron
hea airon
ヘアアイロン

hair dryer
hea doraiyā
ヘアドライヤー

black
kuroi
黒い

barber
rihatsushi
理髪師

bald
hageta
はげた

brown
chairo no
茶色の

shaving cream
**higesoriyō
kuriimu**
ひげそり用
クリーム

mustache
kuchihige
口ひげ

blond
burondo no
ブロンドの

razor
kamisori
かみそり

freckles
sobakasu
そばかす

red
akai
赤い

toenail
ashiyubi no tsume
足指のつめ

beard
agohige
あごひげ

pedicurist
pedikyuashi
ペディキュア師

nail clippers
tsumekiri
つめ切り

nail file
tsumeyasuri
つめやすり

crew cut
kakugari
角刈り

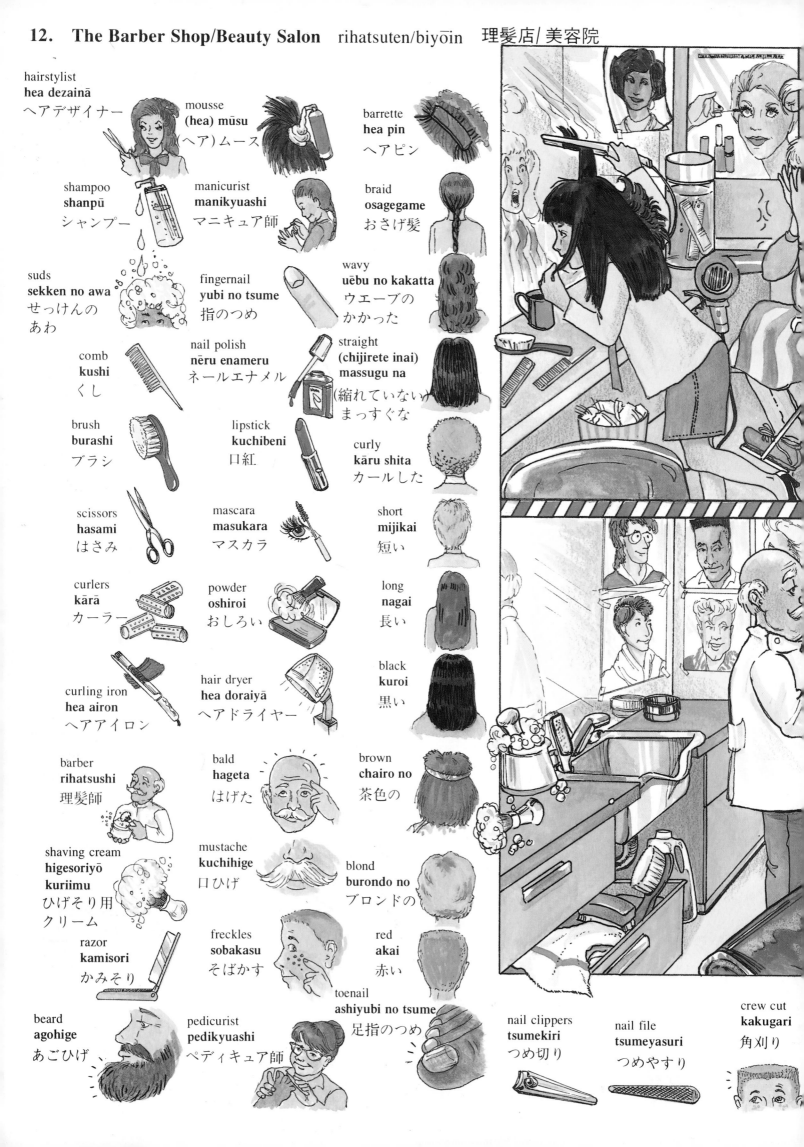

ponytail
poniitēru
ポニーテール

bangs
kirisage maegami
切り下げ前髪

bun
uzumakijō no sokuhatsu
うずまき状の
束髪

part
(tōhatsu no) wakeme
（頭髪の）
分け目

hair spray
hea supurē
ヘアスプレー

hair
tōhatsu
頭髪

blow dryer
hea doraiyā
ヘアドライヤー

13. The Post Office yūbinkyoku 郵便局

packing tape
nizukuriyō tēpu
荷造り用テープ

package
kozutsumi
小包

scale
hakari
はかり

ink pad
sutanpudai
スタンプ台

post-office box
shishobako
私書箱

rubber stamp
gomuin
ゴム印

label
raberu
ラベル

rubber band
wagomu
輪ゴム

letter
tegami
手紙

postcard
hagaki
はがき

string
himo
ひも

knot
musubime
結び目

bow
chōmusubi
ちょう結び

postmark
sutanpu, yūbin no keshiin
スタンプ, 郵便 の 消印

phone booth
denwa bokkusu
電話ボックス

return address
sashidashinin jūsho shimei
差し出し人 住所氏名

mailbox
yūbin posuto
郵便ポスト

address
atena
あて名

mail slot
yūbin sashiireguchi
郵便差し入れ口

zip code
yūbin bangō
郵便番号

postal worker
yūbinkyokuin
郵便局員

mailbag
yūbin haitatsu kaban
郵便配達かばん

stamp
kitte
切手

The Bank ginkō 銀行

paper clip
shorui tome kurippu
書類留めクリップ

security guard
keibiin
警備員

security camera
bōhan kamera
防犯カメラ

safe
kinko
金庫

credit card
kurejitto kādo
クレジットカード

typewriter
taipuraitā
タイプライター

safety deposit box
kashi kinko
貸金庫

notepad
memochō
メモ帳

file cabinet
shorui dana
書類棚

teller
kinsen suitō gakari
金銭出納係

wallet
saifu
さいふ

key
kagi
かぎ

lock
jō
錠

receptionist
uketsuke gakari
受付係

bill
shihei
紙幣

coin
kōka
硬貨

check
kogitte
小切手

checkbook
kogittechō
小切手帳

piggy bank
(buta no) chokinbako
（ぶたの）貯金箱

signature
sain
サイン

drive-in
doraibuin ginkō
ドライブイン銀行

automatic teller
jidō yokin shiharaiki
自動預金支払機

14. At the Gas Station gasorin sutando ガソリンスタンド

mechanic
shūrikō
修理工

coveralls
**tsunagi,
kabarōru**
つなぎ,
カバロール

gas pump
gasorin ponpu
ガソリンポンプ

pliers
penchi
ペンチ

oil
sekiyu
石油

race car
kyōsōyō no kuruma
競走用の車

rag
borokire
ぼろきれ

sunroof
sanrūfu
サンルーフ

dashboard
dasshubōdo
ダッシュボード

garage
garēji
ガレージ

backseat
kōbu no zaseki
後部の座席

tow truck
rekkāsha
レッカー車

car wash
senshajō
洗車場

driver's seat
untenseki
運転席

truck driver
torakku no untenshu
トラックの運転手

gas cap
gasorin no futa
ガソリンのふた

passenger's seat
kyakuseki
客 席

tank truck
tankusha
タンク車

tricycle
sanrinsha
三輪車

seat belt
shiito beruto
シートベルト

bicycle
jitensha
自転車

handlebars
handoru
ハンドル

hood
bonnetto
ボンネット

hand brake
hando burēki
ハンドブレーキ

reflectors
hanshakyō
反射鏡

engine
enjin
エンジン

bicycle chain
chēn
チェーン

pedal
pedaru
ペダル

trunk
toranku
トランク

spokes
**supōku,
(sharin no) ya**
スポーク, (車輪
の) 輻

kickstand
ippon sutando
一本スタンド

fender
fendā, doroyoke
フェンダー,
どろよけ

training wheels
hojorin
補助輪

jack
jakki
ジャッキ

flat tire
panku shita taiya
パンクしたタイヤ

tire
taiya
タイヤ

hubcap
hoiiru kyappu
ホイールキャップ

headlight
heddoraito
ヘッドライ

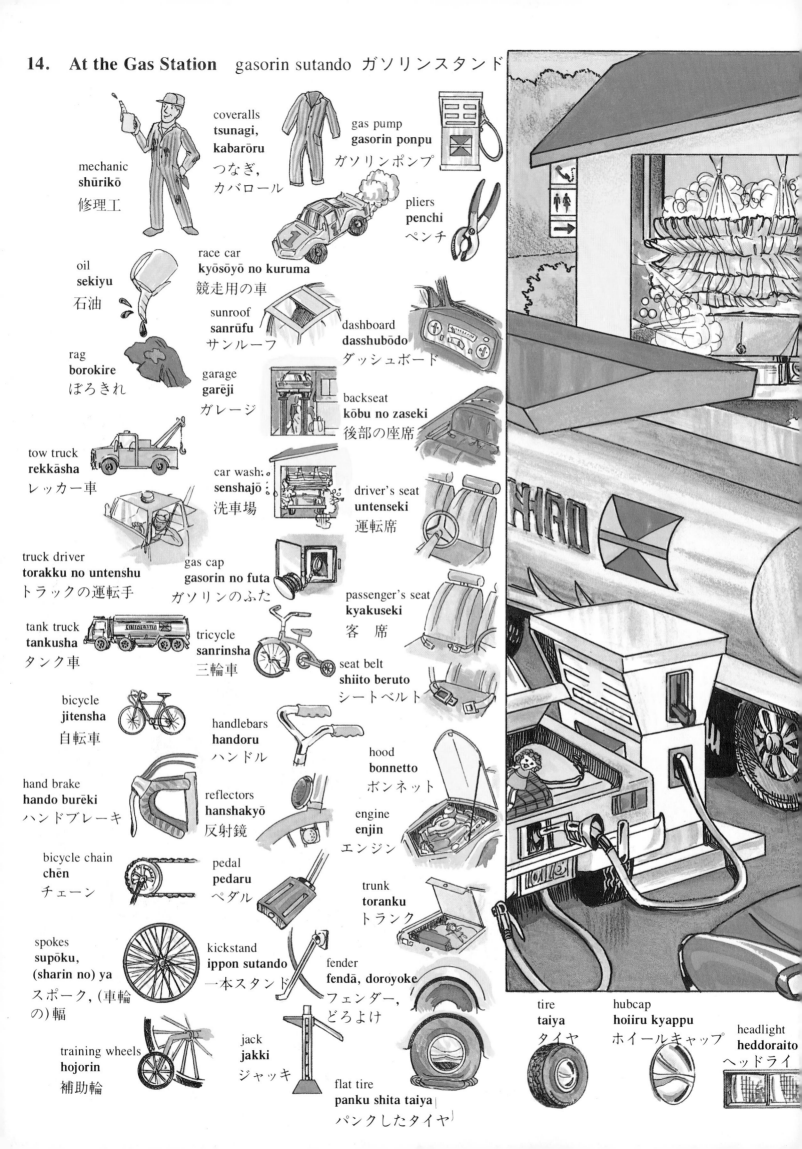

brake lights	windshield	windshield wipers	steering wheel	rearview mirror	air hose	door handle
burēki raito	**furonto garasu**	**waipā**	**handoru**	**bakku mirā**	**ea hōsu**	**doa no totte**
ブレーキライト	フロントガラス	ワイパー	ハンドル	バックミラー	エアホース	ドアの取っ手

saleswoman
onna ten'in, joshi ten'in
女店員

judge
saibankan
裁判官

cook
kokku
コック

model
moderu
モデル

electrician
denkikō
電気工

athlete
supōtsuman
スポーツマン

fire fighter
shōbōshi
消防士

architect
kenchikuka
建築家

doorman
doaman
ドアマン

plumber
kaikankō
配管工

bus driver
basu untenshu
バス運転手

television repairer
terebi shūrikō
テレビ修理工

taxi driver
takushii untenshu
タクシー運転手

fashion designer
fasshon dezainā
ファッション
デザイナー

tour guide
tsuā gaido
ツアーガイド

bookseller
hon'yasan
本屋さん

librarian
shisho
司書

computer programmer
konpyūtā no puroguramā
コンピューターの
プログラマー

photographer
kameraman
カメラマン

gardener
uekiya
植木屋

salesman
danshi ten'in
男子店員

painter
penkiya
ペンキ屋

secretary
hisho
秘書

weather forecaster
tenki yohō gakari
天気予報係

veterinarian
jūi
獣医

policewoman
fujin keikan
婦人警官

disc jockey
disuku jokkii
ディスクジョッキー

reporter
repōtā
レポーター

tailor
yōfukuya
洋服屋

construction worker
kensetsu sagyōin
建設作業員

florist
hanaya
花屋

factory worker
kōin
工員

butcher
nikuyasan
肉屋さん

optician
meganeya
めがね屋

jeweler
hōsekishō
宝石商

foreman
genba kantoku
現場監督

carpenter
daiku
大工

banker
ginkōka
銀行家

artist
gaka
画家

pharmacist
kusuriya
薬屋

sailor
suihei
水兵

lawyer
bengoshi
弁護士

paramedic
kyūkyū taiin
救急隊員

letter carrier
yūbin shūhainin
郵便集配人

fisherman
ryōshi
漁師

cowboy
kaubōi
カウボーイ

policeman
keikan
警官

astronomer
tenmon gakusha
天文学者

16. Going Places (Transportation) yusō kikan 輸送機関

car
jidōsha
自動車

airplane
hikōki
飛行機

jeep
jiipu
ジープ

van
ban
バン

hang glider
hangu guraidā
ハンググライダー

hot-air balloon
nekkikyū
熱気球

scooter
kata ashi sukēto
片足スケート

sail
ho
帆

helicopter
herikoputā
ヘリコプタ

skateboard
sukētobōdo
スケートボード

sailboat
hansen
帆船

rowboat
bōto
ボート

roller skates
rōrā sukēto
ローラースケート

tugboat
tagubōto
タグボート

cruise ship
yūransen
遊覧船

canoe
kanū
カヌー

train
ressha
列車

motorboat
mōtābōto
モーターボート

blimp
kogata hikōsen
小型飛行船

taxi
takushii
タクシー

police car
patokā
パトカー

stroller
bebii kā
ベビーカー

truck
torakku
トラック

camper
kyanpingu kā
キャンピングカー

bicycle
jitensha
自転車

fire engine
shōbōsha
消防車

baby carriage
ubaguruma
うば車

traffic lights
kōtsū shingōki
交通信号機

ambulance
kyūkyūsha
救急車

cement mixer
konkuriito mikisā
コンクリートミキサー

motorcycle
ōtobai
オートバイ

stop!
tomare
止まれ

bus
basu
バス

wait!
mate
待て

lighthouse
tōdai
燈台

go!
susume
進め

school bus
sukūru basu
スクールバス

street
tōri
通り

intersection
kōsaten
交差点

sidewalk
hodō
歩道

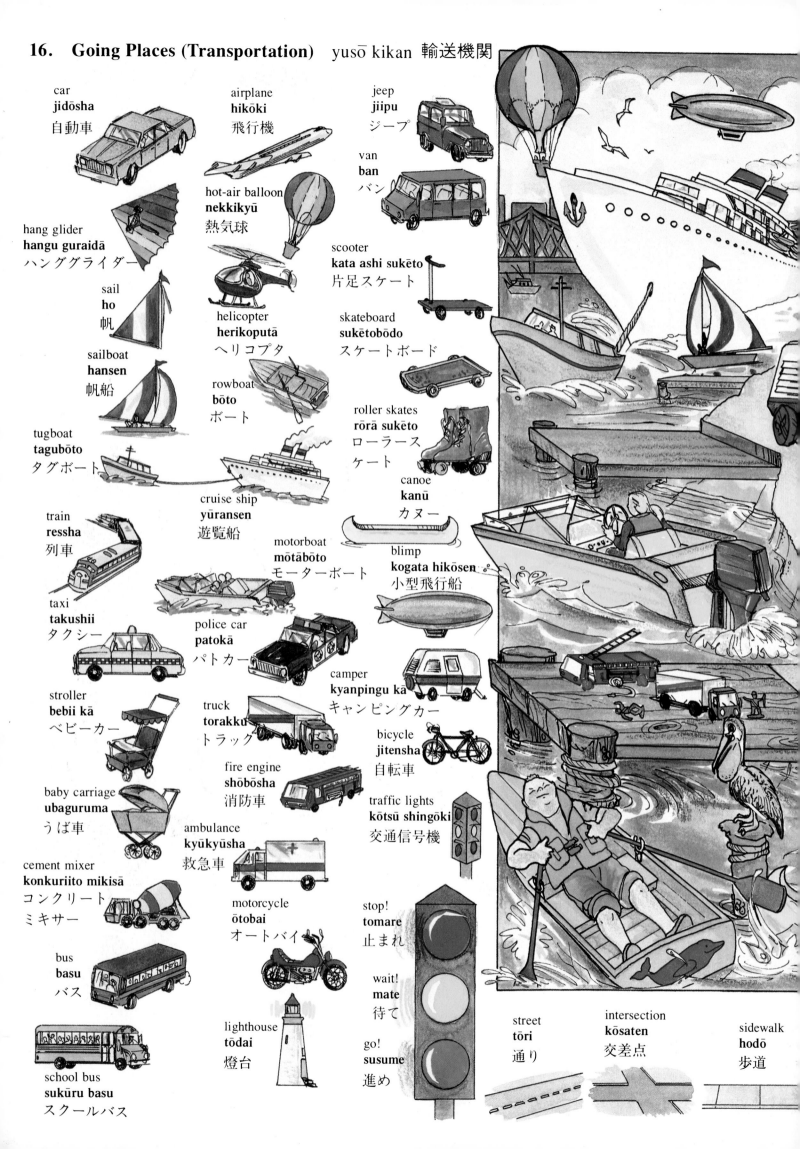

dock
funatsukiba
船着き場

bridge
hashi
橋

crosswalk
ōdan hodō
横断歩道

oar
ōru
オール

boat
bōto
ボート

stop sign
teishi no hyōshiki
停止の標識

17. The Airport　kūkō　空港

pilot
pairotto
パイロット

air-traffic controller
kōkū kanseikan
航空管制官

airplane
hikōki
飛行機

copilot
fuku pairotto
副パイロット
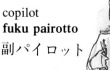

headset
heddohōn
ヘッドホーン

propeller
puropera
プロペラ

navigator
nabigētā
ナヴィゲーター

control tower
kansei tō
管制塔

wing
tsubasa
翼

flight attendant
jōkyaku gakari
乗客係

radar screen
rēdā sukuriin
レーダー
スクリーン

engine
enjin
エンジン

baggage handler
tenimotsu toriatsukainin
手荷物取り
扱い人

flags
hata
旗

landing gear
chakuriku sōchi
着陸装置

porter
pōtā
ポーター

elevator
erebētā
エレベーター

runway
kassōro
滑走路

baggage claim
tenimotsu uketorisho
手荷物受け
取り所

metal detector
kinzoku tanchiki
金属探知器

hangar
kakunōko
格納庫

baggage check-in
tenimotsu chekku
手荷物
チェック

escalator
esukarētā
エスカレーター

concorde
konkorudo
コンコルド

ticket counter
chiketto kauntā
チケット
カウンター

gate
gēto
ゲート

luggage
compartment
tenimotsu dana
手荷物棚

ticket agent
kippu toriatsukainin
切符取扱人
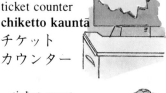

baggage cart
tenimotsu unpansha
手荷物
運搬車

seat
zaseki
座席

ticket
kippu
切符
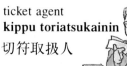

customs officer
zeikanri
税関吏

passenger
jōkyaku
乗客

snack bar
keishokudō
軽食堂

passport
pasupōto
パスポート

video camera
bideo kamera
ビデオカメラ

tennis racket
tenisu no raketto
テニスのラケット

binoculars
sōgankyō
双眼鏡

camera
kamera
カメラ

purse
handobaggu
ハンドバッグ

suitcase
sūtsukēsu
スーツケース

garment bag
ishōire kaban
衣装入れかばん

briefcase
shorui kaban
書類かばん

18. Sports   supōtsu   スポーツ

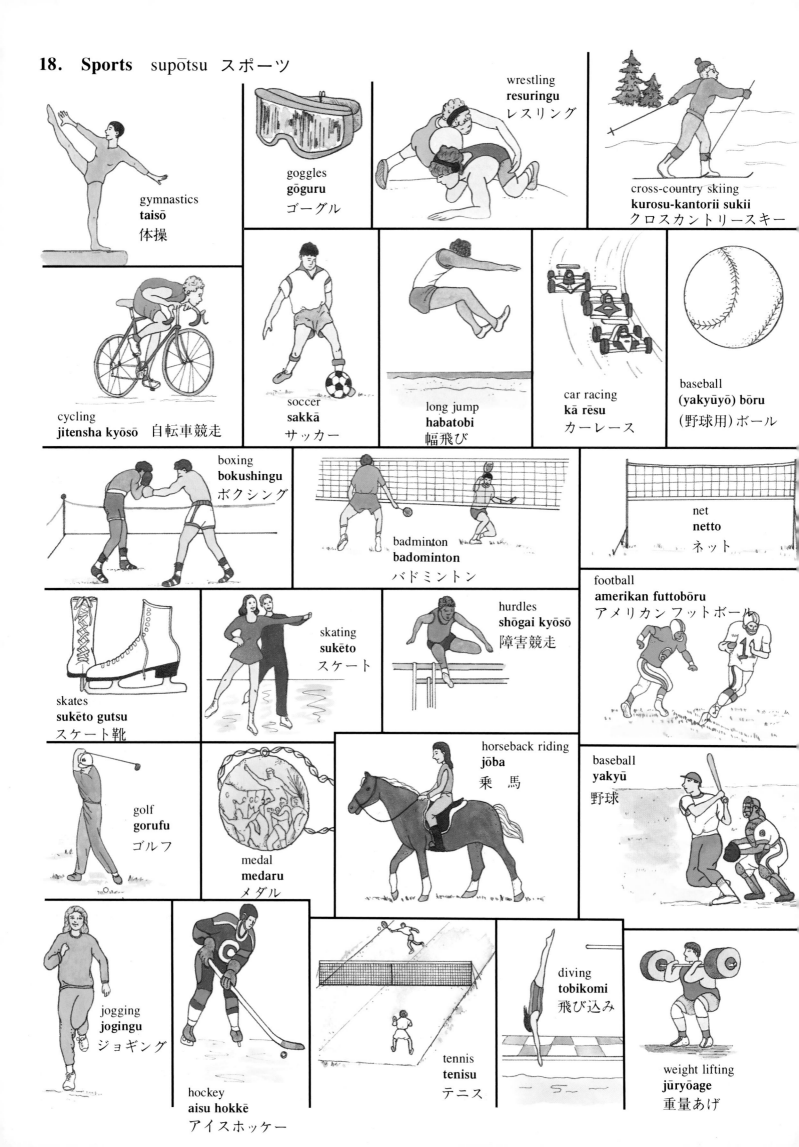

gymnastics
taisō
体操

goggles
gōguru
ゴーグル

wrestling
resuringu
レスリング

cross-country skiing
kurosu-kantorii sukii
クロスカントリースキー

cycling
jitensha kyōsō   自転車競走

soccer
sakkā
サッカー

long jump
habatobi
幅飛び

car racing
kā rēsu
カーレース

baseball
(yakyūyō) bōru
(野球用) ボール

boxing
bokushingu
ボクシング

badminton
badominton
バドミントン

net
netto
ネット

football
amerikan futtobōru
アメリカンフットボール

skates
sukēto gutsu
スケート靴

skating
sukēto
スケート

hurdles
shōgai kyōsō
障害競走

golf
gorufu
ゴルフ

medal
medaru
メダル

horseback riding
jōba
乗　馬

baseball
yakyū
野球

jogging
jogingu
ジョギング

hockey
aisu hokkē
アイスホッケー

tennis
tenisu
テニス

diving
tobikomi
飛び込み

weight lifting
jūryōage
重量あげ

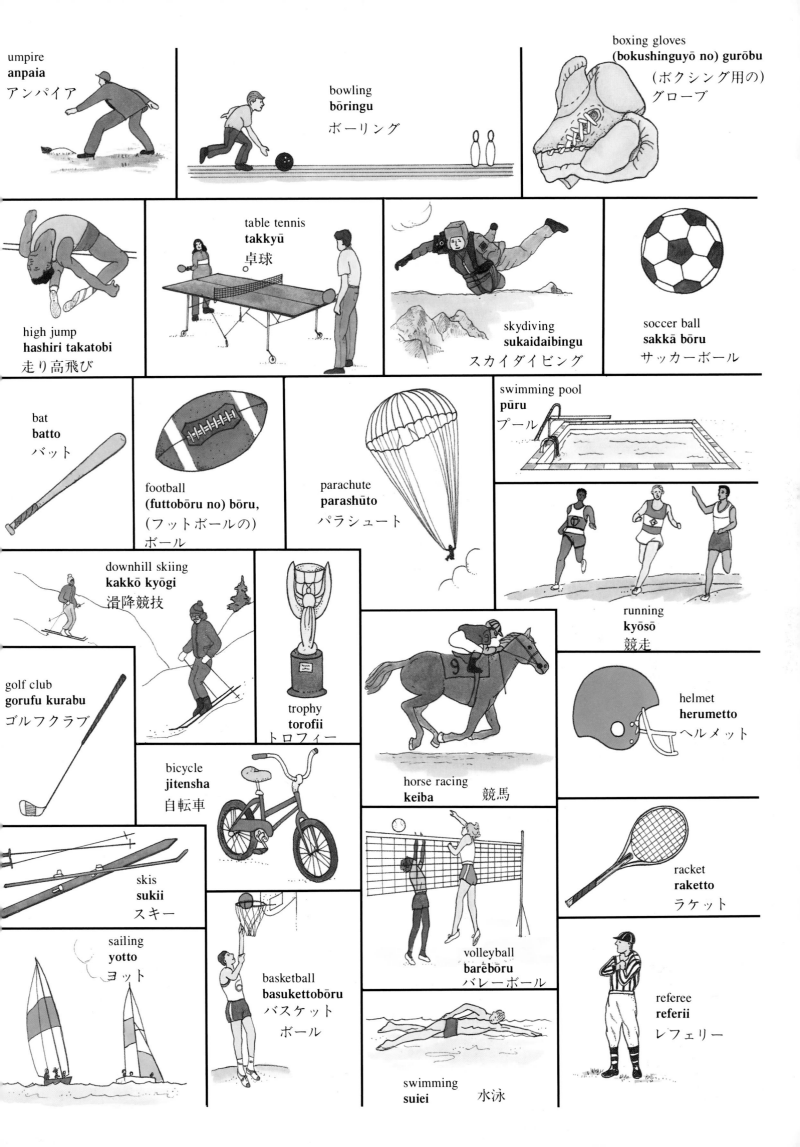

umpire
anpaia
アンパイア

bowling
bōringu
ボーリング

boxing gloves
(bokushinguyō no) gurōbu
（ボクシング用の）
グローブ

high jump
hashiri takatobi
走り高飛び

table tennis
takkyū
卓球

skydiving
sukaidaibingu
スカイダイビング

soccer ball
sakkā bōru
サッカーボール

bat
batto
バット

football
(futtobōru no) bōru,
（フットボールの）
ボール

parachute
parashūto
パラシュート

swimming pool
pūru
プール

downhill skiing
kakkō kyōgi
滑降競技

trophy
torofii
トロフィー

running
kyōsō
競走

golf club
gorufu kurabu
ゴルフクラブ

bicycle
jitensha
自転車

horse racing
keiba　競馬

helmet
herumetto
ヘルメット

skis
sukii
スキー

racket
raketto
ラケット

sailing
yotto
ヨット

basketball
basukettobōru
バスケット
ボール

volleyball
barēbōru
バレーボール

referee
referii
レフェリー

swimming
suiei　水泳

19. The Talent Show   tarento shō   タレントショー

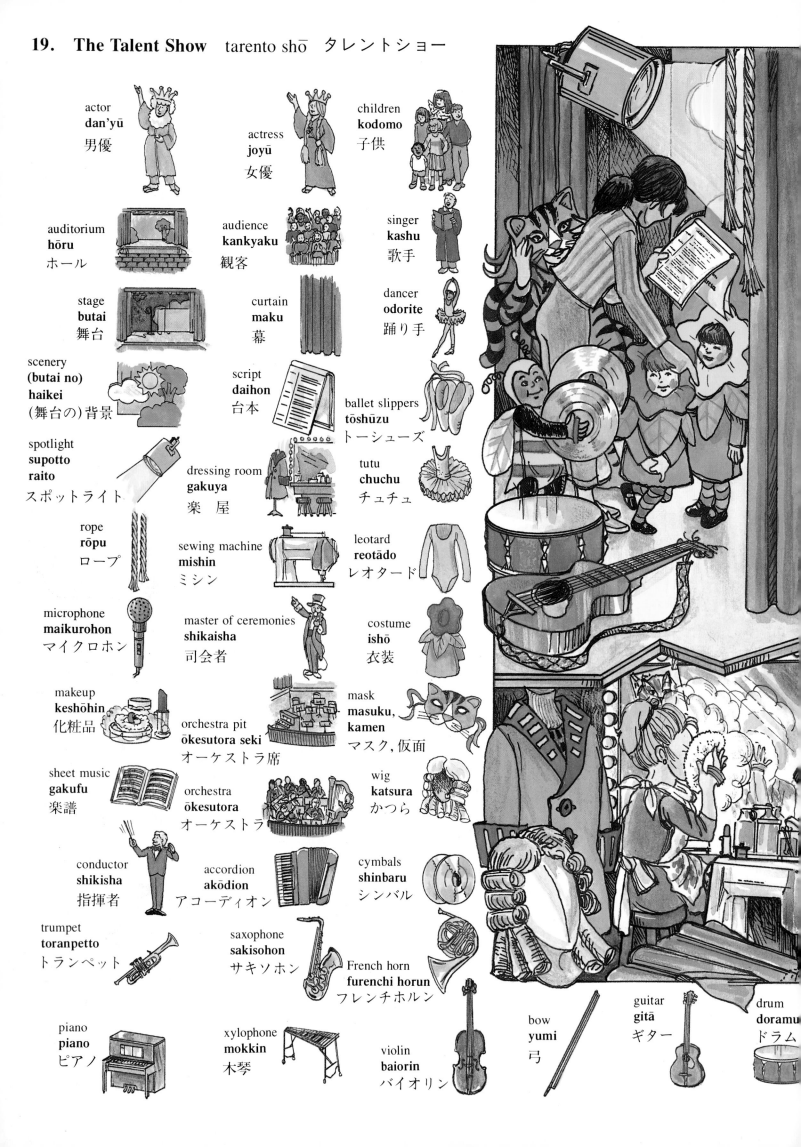

actor
dan'yū
男優

actress
joyū
女優

children
kodomo
子供

auditorium
hōru
ホール

audience
kankyaku
観客

singer
kashu
歌手

stage
butai
舞台

curtain
maku
幕

dancer
odorite
踊り手

scenery
**(butai no)
haikei**
(舞台の)背景

script
daihon
台本

ballet slippers
tōshūzu
トーシューズ

spotlight
**supotto
raito**
スポットライト

dressing room
gakuya
楽屋

tutu
chuchu
チュチュ

rope
rōpu
ロープ

sewing machine
mishin
ミシン

leotard
reotādo
レオタード

microphone
maikurohon
マイクロホン

master of ceremonies
shikaisha
司会者

costume
ishō
衣装

makeup
keshōhin
化粧品

orchestra pit
ōkesutora seki
オーケストラ席

mask
**masuku,
kamen**
マスク, 仮面

sheet music
gakufu
楽譜

orchestra
ōkesutora
オーケストラ

wig
katsura
かつら

conductor
shikisha
指揮者

accordion
akōdion
アコーディオン

cymbals
shinbaru
シンバル

trumpet
toranpetto
トランペット

saxophone
sakisohon
サキソホン

French horn
furenchi horun
フレンチホルン

piano
piano
ピアノ

xylophone
mokkin
木琴

violin
baiorin
バイオリン

bow
yumi
弓

guitar
gitā
ギター

drum
doramu
ドラム

| | tuba
chūba
チューバ | | flute
furūto
フルート | | trombone
toronbōn
トロンボーン | | clarinet
kurarinetto
クラリネット | | cello
chero
チェロ | | strings
gen
弦 | | harp
hāpu
ハープ |

20. At the Zoo dōbutsuen 動物園

zookeeper
shiiku gakari
飼育係

rhinoceros
sai
さい

lion
raion
ライオン

tiger
tora
とら

tiger cub
tora no ko
とらの子

jaguar
jagā
ジャガー

leopard
hyō
ひょう

flamingo
furamingo
フラミンゴ

owl
fukurō
ふくろう

swan
hakuchō
白鳥

penguin
pengin
ペンギン

peacock
**(osu no)
kujaku**
（雄の）
くじゃく

eagle
washi
わし

elephant
zō
象

ostrich
dachō
だちょう

bear
kuma
くま

bear cub
koguma
子ぐま

polar bear
shirokuma
白くま

panda
panda
パンダ

gorilla
gorira
ゴリラ

parrot
ōmu
おうむ

snake
hebi
へび

seal
azarashi
あざらし

walrus
seiuchi
せいうち

hump
(rakuda no) kobu
（らくだの）
こぶ

camel
rakuda
らくだ

animals
dōbutsu
動物

fox
kitsune
きつね

wolf
ōkami
おおかみ

alligator
arigētā, wani
アリゲー
ター，わに

zebra
shimauma
しま馬

giraffe
kirin
きりん

monkey
saru
さる

hippopotamus
kaba
かば

kangaroo
kangarū
カンガルー

deer
shika
しか

lizard
tokage
とかげ

turtle
umigame
海がめ

horns
tsuno
角

wings
hane, tsubasa
羽，翼

feathers
umō
羽毛

beak
kuchibashi
くちばし

paw
ashi
足

claws
tsume
つめ

mane
tategami
たてがみ

tail
o
尾

hoof
hizume
ひづめ

stripes
shima
しま

spots
hanten
はん点

21. At the Circus sākasu サーカス

clown
piero
ピエロ

popcorn
poppukōn
ポップコーン

caramel apple
ringoame
りんごあめ

balloon
gomu fūsen
ゴム風船

peanuts
piinatsu
ピーナツ

film
firumu
フィルム

magician
tejinashi
手品師

lion
raion
ライオン

tent pole
tentoyō shichū
テント用支柱

elephant
zō
象

flashbulb
sutorobo
ストロボ

camera
kamera
カメラ

juggler
kyokugeishi
曲芸師

tickets
nyūjōken
入場券

baton
baton
バトン

turban
tāban
ターバン

light bulb
denkyū
電球

night
yoru
夜

ticket booth
nyūjōken uriba
入場券売場

stilts
takeuma
竹馬

big top
sākasu no daitento
サーカスの
大テント

circus parade
**sākasu no
kaomise gyōretsu**
サーカスの顔見
せ行列

rest rooms
toire
トイレ

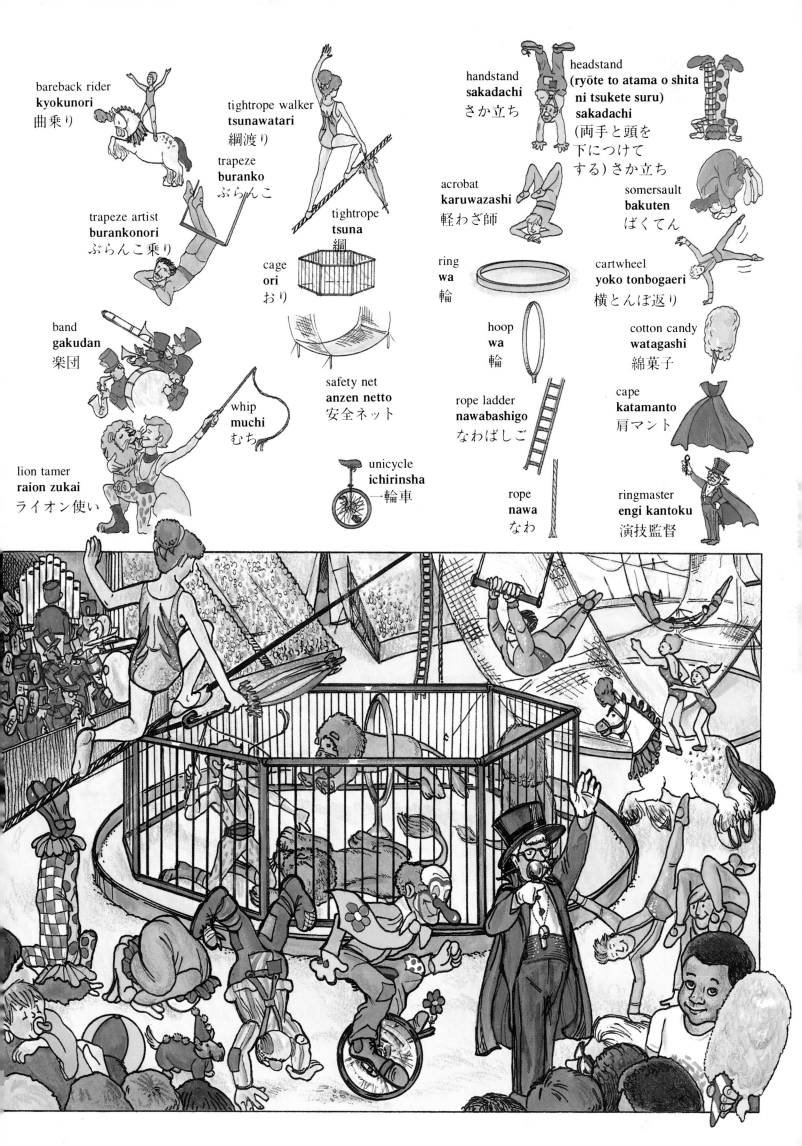

bareback rider
kyokunori
曲乗り

tightrope walker
tsunawatari
綱渡り

trapeze
buranko
ぶらんこ

trapeze artist
burankonori
ぶらんこ乗り

tightrope
tsuna
綱

cage
ori
おり

band
gakudan
楽団

whip
muchi
むち

safety net
anzen netto
安全ネット

lion tamer
raion zukai
ライオン使い

unicycle
ichirinsha
一輪車

handstand
sakadachi
さか立ち

headstand
**(ryōte to atama o shita
ni tsukete suru)
sakadachi**
（両手と頭を
下につけて
する）さか立ち

acrobat
karuwazashi
軽わざ師

somersault
bakuten
ばくてん

ring
wa
輪

cartwheel
yoko tonbogaeri
横とんぼ返り

hoop
wa
輪

cotton candy
watagashi
綿菓子

rope ladder
nawabashigo
なわばしご

cape
katamanto
肩マント

rope
nawa
なわ

ringmaster
engi kantoku
演技監督

scuba diver
sukyuba daibā
スキュバ
ダイバー

wet suit
uetto sūtsu
ウエット
スーツ

flipper
ashihire
足ひれ

oxygen tank
sanso bonbe
酸素ボンベ

snorkel
shunōkeru
シュノーケル

mask
**masuku,
suichū megane**
マスク，水中 めがね

starfish
hitode
ひとで

jellyfish
kurage
くらげ

sea turtle
umigame
うみがめ

lobster
robusutā
ロブスター

stingray
akaei
あかえい

dolphin
iruka
いるか

shark
same, fuka
さめ，ふか

octopus
tako
たこ

tentacle
shokushu
触手

swordfish
mekajiki
めかじき

angelfish
enzerufisshu
エンゼルフィッシュ

school (of fish)
mure
群れ

fishing line
tsuri ito
つり糸

fishhook
tsuribari
つり針

buoy
bui
ブイ

submarine
sensuikan
潜水艦

porthole
gensō
舷窓

sea urchin
uni
うに

sea horse
tatsu no otoshigo
たつのおとしご

seaweed
kaisō
海草

shipwreck
nanpasen
難破船

helm
kaji
かじ

cannon
taihō
大砲

anchor
ikari
いかり

treasure chest
hōsekibako
宝石箱

treasure
zaihō
財宝

gold
kinka
金貨

silver
ginka
銀貨

jewel
hōseki
宝石

barnacle
fujitsubo
ふじつぼ

coral
sango
さんご

coral reef
sangoshō
さんご礁

seashell
kai
貝

wave
nami
波

sand
sunahama
砂浜

bubble
awa, kihō
あわ，気泡

scales
uroko
うろこ

gills
era
えら

fin
hire
ひれ

clam
hamaguri
はまぐり

crab
kani
かに

squid
yariika
やりいか

whale
kujira
鯨

23. Space uchū 宇宙

astronaut
uchū hikōshi
宇宙飛行士

space suit
uchū fuku
宇宙服

space helmet
uchū herumetto
宇宙ヘル
メット

footprint
ashiato
足跡

space walk
uchū yūei
宇宙遊泳

moon rock
tsuki no ishi
月の石

space shuttle
supēsu shatoru
スペースシャトル

lunar rover
getsumensha
月面車

laboratory
kenkyūshitsu
研究室

cargo bay
nimotsu shitsu
荷物室
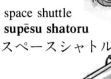

landing capsule
chakuriku kapuseru
着陸カプ
セル

scientist
kagakusha
科学者

control panel
seigyo ban
制御盤

ladder
hashigo
はしご

lab coat
jikkengi
実験着

satellite
jinkō eisei
人工衛星

space station
uchū sutēshon
宇宙ステーション

microscope
kenbikyō
顕微鏡

computer
konpyūta
コンピューター

spaceship
uchūsen
宇宙船

solar panel
taiyō denchiban
太陽電池板

alien
uchūjin
宇宙人

meteor shower
ryūseiu
流星雨

beaker
biikā
ビーカー

antenna
antena
アンテナ

constellation
seiza
星座

test tube
shikenkan
試験管

asteroid
shōwakusei
小惑星

solar system
taiyōkei
太陽系

galaxy
gingakei
銀河系

earth
chikyū
地球

moon
tsuki
月

sun
taiyō
太陽

planet	rings	crater	stars	comet	nebula	rocket
wakusei	**(wakusei no) wa**	**kurētā**	**hoshi**	**suisei**	**seiun**	**roketto**
惑星	（惑星の）輪	クレーター	星	すい星	星雲	ロケット

robot
robotto
ロボット

24. Human History jinrui no rekishi 人類の歴史

rock
iwa
岩

boulder
**maruishi,
gyokuseki**
丸石，玉石

bone
hone
骨

insect
konchū
こん虫

fern
shida
しだ

tree
ki
木

cave
hora ana
ほら穴

fur
kegawa
毛皮

fire
hi
火

stick
bōkire
棒切れ

wheel
sharin
車輪

flint
hiuchi ishi
火打ち石

arrowhead
yajiri
矢じり

club
konbō
こん棒

spear
yari
やり

mammoth
manmosu
マンモス

tusk
kiba
きば

trunk
hana
鼻

bison
baison
バイソン

paint
enogu
絵の具

cave drawing
hora ana kaiga
洞穴絵画

hut
koya
小屋

corn
tōmorokoshi
とうもろこし

wheat
komugi
小麦

weaver
oru hito
織る人

loom
shokki
織機

kiln
kama, ro
かま，炉

potter
tōkō
陶工

pot
tsubo
つぼ

clay
nendo
粘土

cart
niguruma
荷車

basket
zaru
ざる

leather
kawa
皮

fishing
gyorō, tsuri
漁労

hunter
kariudo
狩人

well
ido
井戸

bucket
baketsu
バケツ

water
mizu
水

cloth
nuno
布

saber-toothed tiger
kenshi tora
剣歯とら

crop
sakumotsu
作物

village
sonraku
村落

cave dwellers
ana kyojin
穴居人

skeleton
kokkaku
骨格

dinosaur
kyōryū
恐竜

pterodactyl
yokuryū
翼竜

ld
take
]

25. The Make-Believe Castle maboroshi no oshiro まぼろしのお城

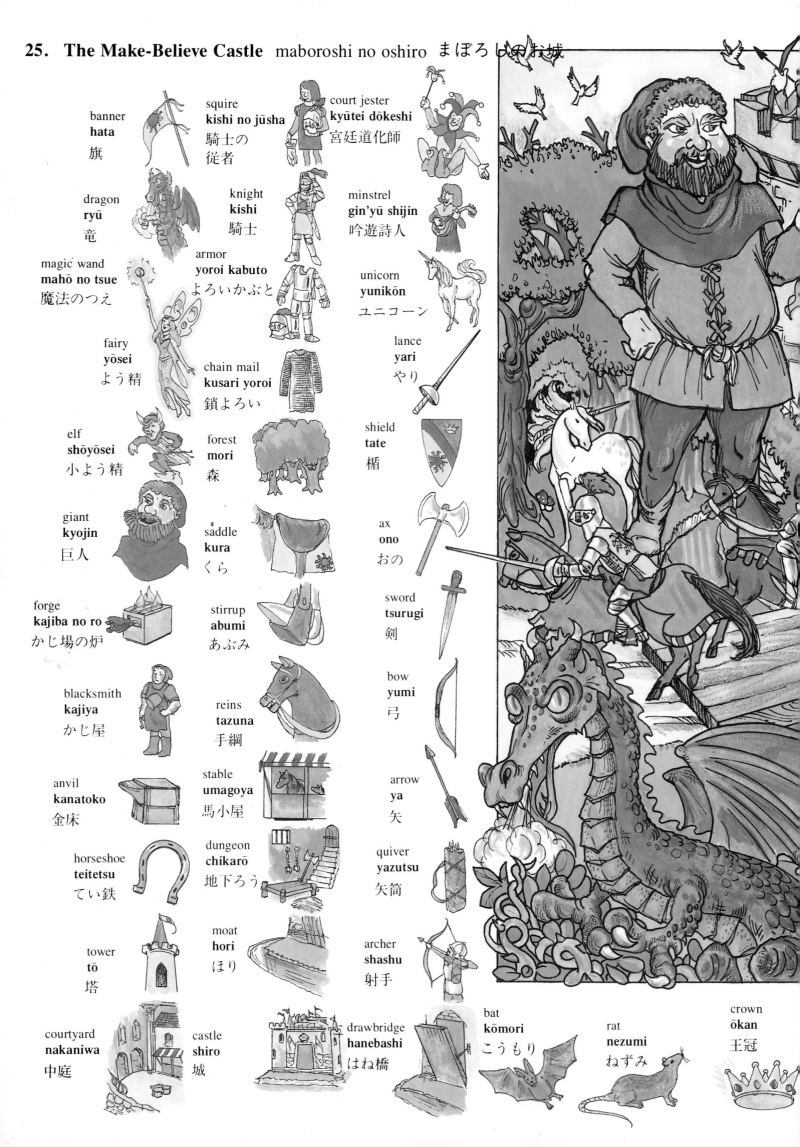

banner
hata
旗

squire
kishi no jūsha
騎士の
従者

court jester
kyūtei dōkeshi
宮廷道化師

dragon
ryū
竜

knight
kishi
騎士

minstrel
gin'yū shijin
吟遊詩人

magic wand
mahō no tsue
魔法のつえ

armor
yoroi kabuto
よろいかぶと

unicorn
yunikōn
ユニコーン

fairy
yōsei
よう精

chain mail
kusari yoroi
鎖よろい

lance
yari
やり

elf
shōyōsei
小よう精

forest
mori
森

shield
tate
楯

giant
kyojin
巨人

saddle
kura
くら

ax
ono
おの

forge
kajiba no ro
かじ場の炉

stirrup
abumi
あぶみ

sword
tsurugi
剣

blacksmith
kajiya
かじ屋

reins
tazuna
手綱

bow
yumi
弓

anvil
kanatoko
金床

stable
umagoya
馬小屋

arrow
ya
矢

horseshoe
teitetsu
てい鉄

dungeon
chikarō
地下ろう

quiver
yazutsu
矢筒

tower
tō
塔

moat
hori
ほり

archer
shashu
射手

courtyard
nakaniwa
中庭

castle
shiro
城

drawbridge
hanebashi
はね橋

bat
kōmori
こうもり

rat
nezumi
ねずみ

crown
ōkan
王冠

king
ō
王

queen
joō
女王

princess
ōjo
王女

prince
ōji
王子

throne
gyokuza
玉座

spider
kumo
くも

spiderweb
kumo no su
くもの巣

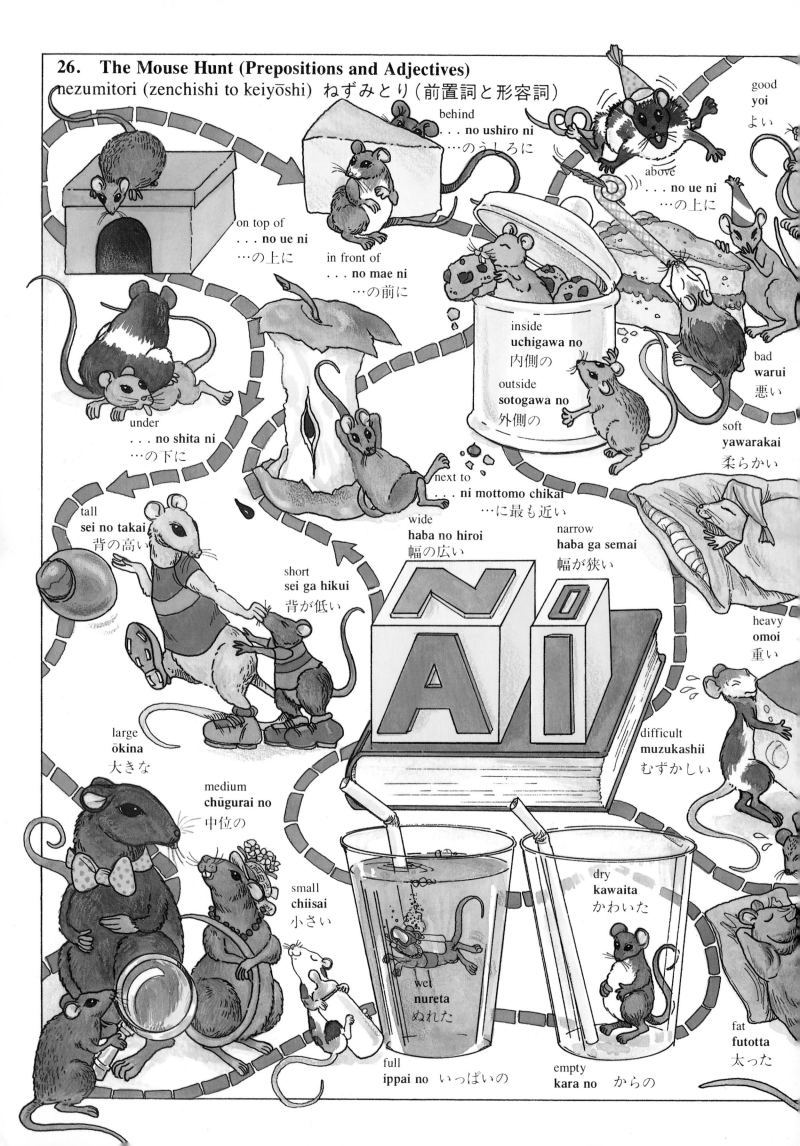

good
yoi
よい

behind
. . . no ushiro ni
…のうしろに

above
. . . no ue ni
…の上に

on top of
. . . no ue ni
…の上に

in front of
. . . no mae ni
…の前に

inside
uchigawa no
内側の

outside
sotogawa no
外側の

bad
warui
悪い

soft
yawarakai
柔らかい

under
. . . no shita ni
…の下に

next to
. . . ni mottomo chikai
…に最も近い

tall
sei no takai
背の高い

short
sei ga hikui
背が低い

wide
haba no hiroi
幅の広い

narrow
haba ga semai
幅が狭い

heavy
omoi
重い

large
ōkina
大きな

difficult
muzukashii
むずかしい

medium
chūgurai no
中位の

small
chiisai
小さい

dry
kawaita
かわいた

wet
nureta
ぬれた

fat
futotta
太った

full
ippai no　いっぱいの

empty
kara no　からの

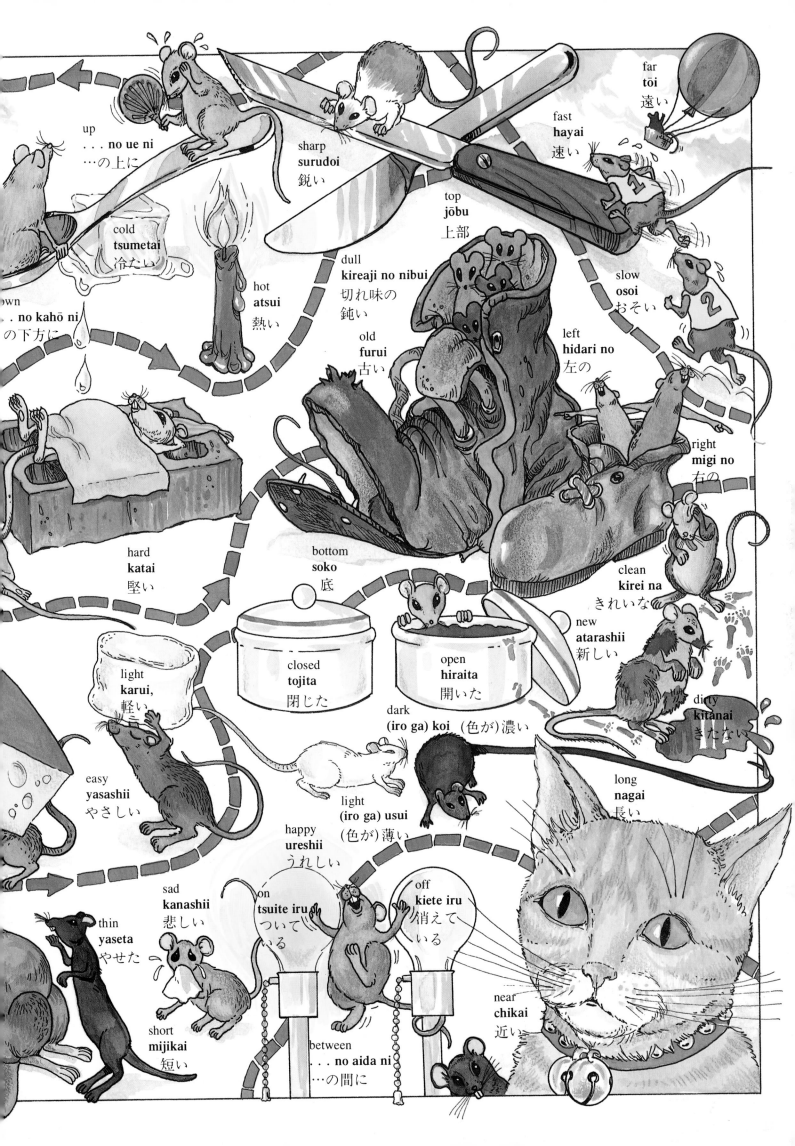

up
...no ue ni
…の上に

sharp
surudoi
鋭い

cold
tsumetai
冷たい

hot
atsui
熱い

dull
kireaji no nibui
切れ味の
鈍い

top
jōbu
上部

fast
hayai
速い

far
tōi
遠い

slow
osoi
おそい

...own
. no kahō ni
…の下方に

old
furui
古い

left
hidari no
左の

right
migi no
右の

hard
katai
堅い

bottom
soko
底

clean
kirei na
きれいな

new
atarashii
新しい

light
karui,
軽い

closed
tojita
閉じた

open
hiraita
開いた

dirty
kitanai
きたない

easy
yasashii
やさしい

dark
(iro ga) koi （色が）濃い

light
(iro ga) usui
（色が）薄い

long
nagai
長い

happy
ureshii
うれしい

sad
kanashii
悲しい

on
tsuite iru
ついて
いる

off
kiete iru
消えて
いる

thin
yaseta
やせた

short
mijikai
短い

between
. . . no aida ni
…の間に

near
chikai
近い

27. Action Words dōsa 動作

drink **nomu** 飲む   eat **taberu** 食べる

sleep **nemuru** 眠る

wash **arau** 洗う

skate **sukēto o suru** スケートをする

fall **korobu** ころぶ

cry **naku** 泣く

laugh **warau** 笑う

fly **tobu** 飛ぶ

write **kaku** 書く

read **yomu** 読む

play (a game) **(gēmu o) suru**; (an instrument) **(gakki o) ensō suru**
（ゲームを）する　　　　（楽器を）演奏する

sit down **suwaru** すわる

stand up **tachiagaru** 立ち上がる

dance **odoru** 踊る

walk **aruku** 歩く

run **hashiru** 走る

climb **noboru** 登る

jump **tobikoeru** 飛び越え

drive **unten suru** 運転する

push **osu** 押す

sell **uru** 売る

buy **kau** 買う

ski **sukii o suru** スキーをする

dive **tobikomu** 飛び込む

swim **oyogu** 泳ぐ

paint **(enogu de) e o kaku** （絵の具で）絵をかく

draw **(sen de) e o kaku** （線で）絵をかく

ride a bicycle **jitensha ni noru** 自転車に乗る

come
kuru
来る

go
iku
行く

throw
nageru 投げる

catch
ukeru 受ける

watch
miharu 見張る

sing
utau 歌う

talk
hanasu 話す

kick
keru ける

listen (to)
kiku 聞く

think
kangaeru 考える

roar
hoeru ほえる

dig
horu 掘る

pour
mizu o yaru 水をやる

juggle
kyokugei o suru
曲芸をする

point (at)
. . . o sasu …をさす

look for
sagasu 捜す

find
mitsukeru 見つける

give
ataeru 与える

receive
morau もらう

cut
kiru
切る

cook
ryōri suru 料理する

open
akeru 開ける

close
shimeru しめる

take a bath
nyūyoku suru 入浴する

teach
oshieru 教える

break
kowasu こわす

fix
shūri suru 修理する

carry
hakobu 運ぶ

pull
hiku 引く

wait
matsu 待つ

28. Colors iro 色

white **shiro** 白

black **kuro** 黒

gray **haiiro** 灰色

red **aka** 赤

purple **murasaki iro** 紫色

yellow **kiiro** 黄色

green **midori** 緑

pink **pinku** ピンク

orange **orenji iro** オレンジ色

brown **chairo** 茶色

blue **aoiro** 青色

gold **kin'iro** 金色

silver **gin'iro** 銀色

29. The Family Tree ikka no keizu 一家の系図

grandmother, grandma **sobo obāchan** 祖母 おばあちゃん

father, dad **chichi, otōsan** 父, おとうさん

mother, mom **haha, okāsan** 母, おかあさん

son **musuko** むすこ

brother **ani, otōto** 兄, 弟

sister **ane, imōto** 姉, 妹

grandfather, grandpa
sofu **ojiichan**
祖父　おじいちゃん

uncle
oji
おじ

aunt
oba
おば

cousin
itoko
いとこ

cousin
itoko
いとこ

daughter
musume
娘

30. Shapes　katachi　形

square
seihōkei
正方形

triangle
sankakukei
三角形

circle
maru
円

rectangle
chōhōkei
長方形

oval
daenkei
だ円形

cube
rippōtai
立方体

octagon
hakkakukei
八角形

sphere
kyū
球

cylinder
enchū
円柱

cone
ensuikei
円すい形

31. Numbers sū 数

Ordinal Numbers
josū
序数

- tenth **jūbanme** 十番目
- ninth **kyūbanme** 九番目
- eighth **hachibanme** 八番目
- seventh **nanabanme, shichibanme** 七番目
- sixth **rokubanme** 六番目
- fifth **gobanme** 五番目
- fourth **yonbanme** 四番目
- third **sanbanme** 三番目
- second **nibanme** 二番目
- first **ichibanme** 一番目

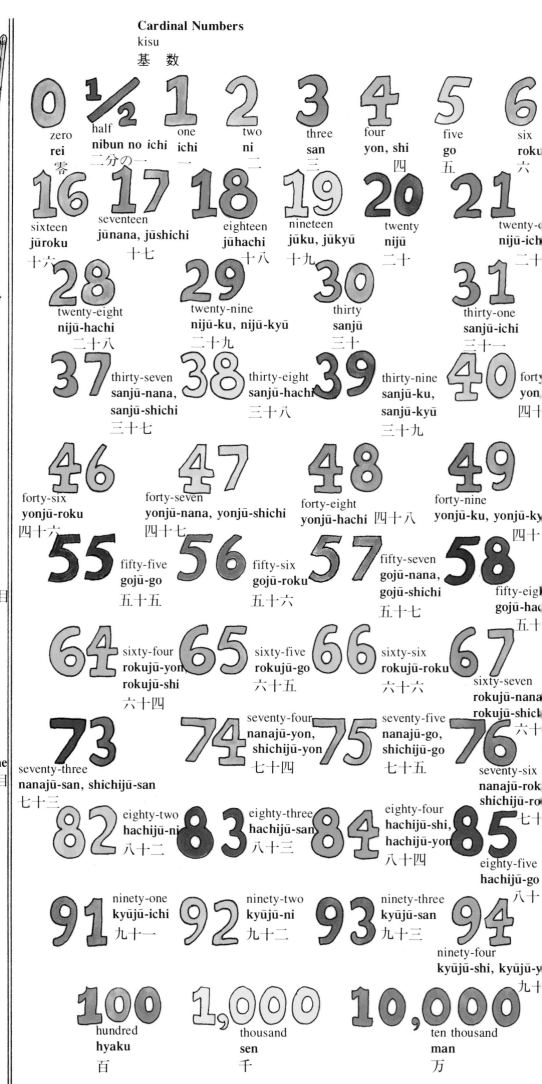

Cardinal Numbers
kisu
基数

- 0 zero **rei** 零
- ½ half **nibun no ichi** 二分の一
- 1 one **ichi** 一
- 2 two **ni** 二
- 3 three **san** 三
- 4 four **yon, shi** 四
- 5 five **go** 五
- 6 six **roku** 六
- 16 sixteen **jūroku** 十六
- 17 seventeen **jūnana, jūshichi** 十七
- 18 eighteen **jūhachi** 十八
- 19 nineteen **jūku, jūkyū** 十九
- 20 twenty **nijū** 二十
- 21 twenty-one **nijū-ichi** 二十一
- 28 twenty-eight **nijū-hachi** 二十八
- 29 twenty-nine **nijū-ku, nijū-kyū** 二十九
- 30 thirty **sanjū** 三十
- 31 thirty-one **sanjū-ichi** 三十一
- 37 thirty-seven **sanjū-nana, sanjū-shichi** 三十七
- 38 thirty-eight **sanjū-hachi** 三十八
- 39 thirty-nine **sanjū-ku, sanjū-kyū** 三十九
- 40 forty **yon** 四十
- 46 forty-six **yonjū-roku** 四十六
- 47 forty-seven **yonjū-nana, yonjū-shichi** 四十七
- 48 forty-eight **yonjū-hachi** 四十八
- 49 forty-nine **yonjū-ku, yonjū-kyū** 四十九
- 55 fifty-five **gojū-go** 五十五
- 56 fifty-six **gojū-roku** 五十六
- 57 fifty-seven **gojū-nana, gojū-shichi** 五十七
- 58 fifty-eight **gojū-hachi** 五十八
- 64 sixty-four **rokujū-yon, rokujū-shi** 六十四
- 65 sixty-five **rokujū-go** 六十五
- 66 sixty-six **rokujū-roku** 六十六
- 67 sixty-seven **rokujū-nana, rokujū-shichi** 六十七
- 73 seventy-three **nanajū-san, shichijū-san** 七十三
- 74 seventy-four **nanajū-yon, shichijū-yon** 七十四
- 75 seventy-five **nanajū-go, shichijū-go** 七十五
- 76 seventy-six **nanajū-roku, shichijū-roku** 七十六
- 82 eighty-two **hachijū-ni** 八十二
- 83 eighty-three **hachijū-san** 八十三
- 84 eighty-four **hachijū-shi, hachijū-yon** 八十四
- 85 eighty-five **hachijū-go** 八十五
- 91 ninety-one **kyūjū-ichi** 九十一
- 92 ninety-two **kyūjū-ni** 九十二
- 93 ninety-three **kyūjū-san** 九十三
- 94 ninety-four **kyūjū-shi, kyūjū-yon** 九十四
- 100 hundred **hyaku** 百
- 1,000 thousand **sen** 千
- 10,000 ten thousand **man** 万

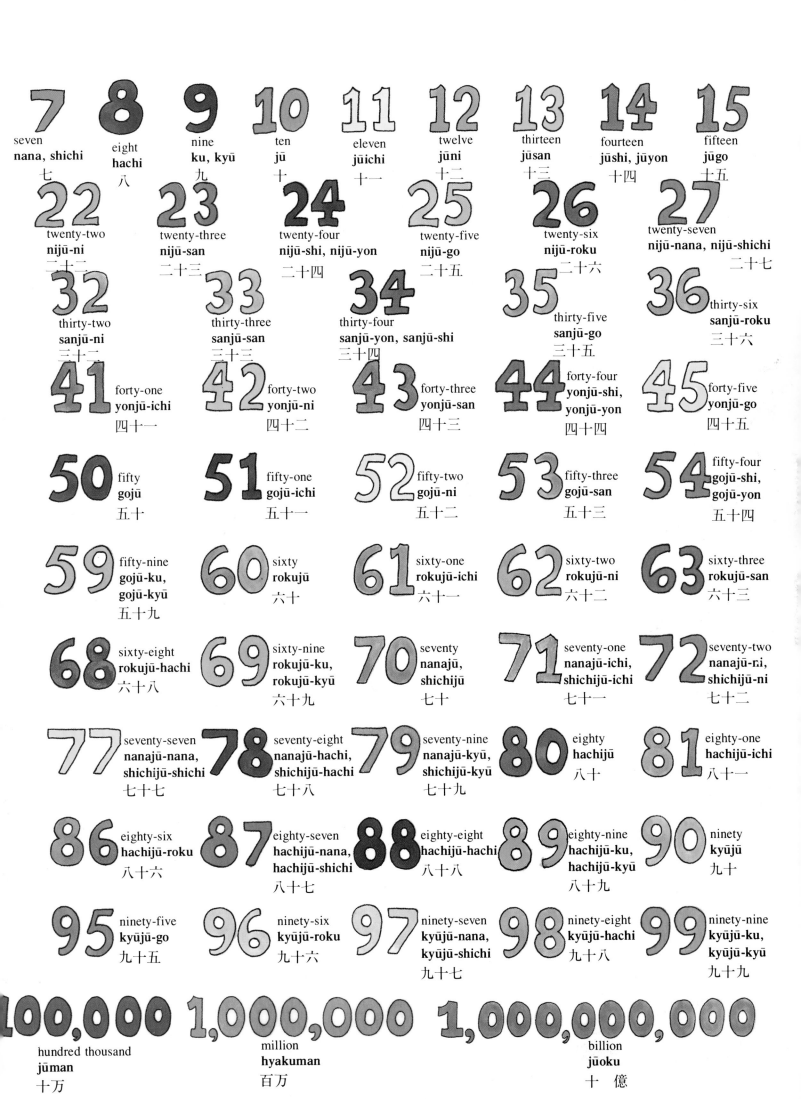

7 seven — nana, shichi — 七
8 eight — hachi — 八
9 nine — ku, kyū — 九
10 ten — jū — 十
11 eleven — jūichi — 十一
12 twelve — jūni — 十二
13 thirteen — jūsan — 十三
14 fourteen — jūshi, jūyon — 十四
15 fifteen — jūgo — 十五

22 twenty-two — nijū-ni — 二十二
23 twenty-three — nijū-san — 二十三
24 twenty-four — nijū-shi, nijū-yon — 二十四
25 twenty-five — nijū-go — 二十五
26 twenty-six — nijū-roku — 二十六
27 twenty-seven — nijū-nana, nijū-shichi — 二十七

32 thirty-two — sanjū-ni — 三十二
33 thirty-three — sanjū-san — 三十三
34 thirty-four — sanjū-yon, sanjū-shi — 三十四
35 thirty-five — sanjū-go — 三十五
36 thirty-six — sanjū-roku — 三十六

41 forty-one — yonjū-ichi — 四十一
42 forty-two — yonjū-ni — 四十二
43 forty-three — yonjū-san — 四十三
44 forty-four — yonjū-shi, yonjū-yon — 四十四
45 forty-five — yonjū-go — 四十五

50 fifty — gojū — 五十
51 fifty-one — gojū-ichi — 五十一
52 fifty-two — gojū-ni — 五十二
53 fifty-three — gojū-san — 五十三
54 fifty-four — gojū-shi, gojū-yon — 五十四

59 fifty-nine — gojū-ku, gojū-kyū — 五十九
60 sixty — rokujū — 六十
61 sixty-one — rokujū-ichi — 六十一
62 sixty-two — rokujū-ni — 六十二
63 sixty-three — rokujū-san — 六十三

68 sixty-eight — rokujū-hachi — 六十八
69 sixty-nine — rokujū-ku, rokujū-kyū — 六十九
70 seventy — nanajū, shichijū — 七十
71 seventy-one — nanajū-ichi, shichijū-ichi — 七十一
72 seventy-two — nanajū-ni, shichijū-ni — 七十二

77 seventy-seven — nanajū-nana, shichijū-shichi — 七十七
78 seventy-eight — nanajū-hachi, shichijū-hachi — 七十八
79 seventy-nine — nanajū-kyū, shichijū-kyū — 七十九
80 eighty — hachijū — 八十
81 eighty-one — hachijū-ichi — 八十一

86 eighty-six — hachijū-roku — 八十六
87 eighty-seven — hachijū-nana, hachijū-shichi — 八十七
88 eighty-eight — hachijū-hachi — 八十八
89 eighty-nine — hachijū-ku, hachijū-kyū — 八十九
90 ninety — kyūjū — 九十

95 ninety-five — kyūjū-go — 九十五
96 ninety-six — kyūjū-roku — 九十六
97 ninety-seven — kyūjū-nana, kyūjū-shichi — 九十七
98 ninety-eight — kyūjū-hachi — 九十八
99 ninety-nine — kyūjū-ku, kyūjū-kyū — 九十九

100,000 hundred thousand — **jūman** — 十万
1,000,000 million — **hyakuman** — 百万
1,000,000,000 billion — **jūoku** — 十億

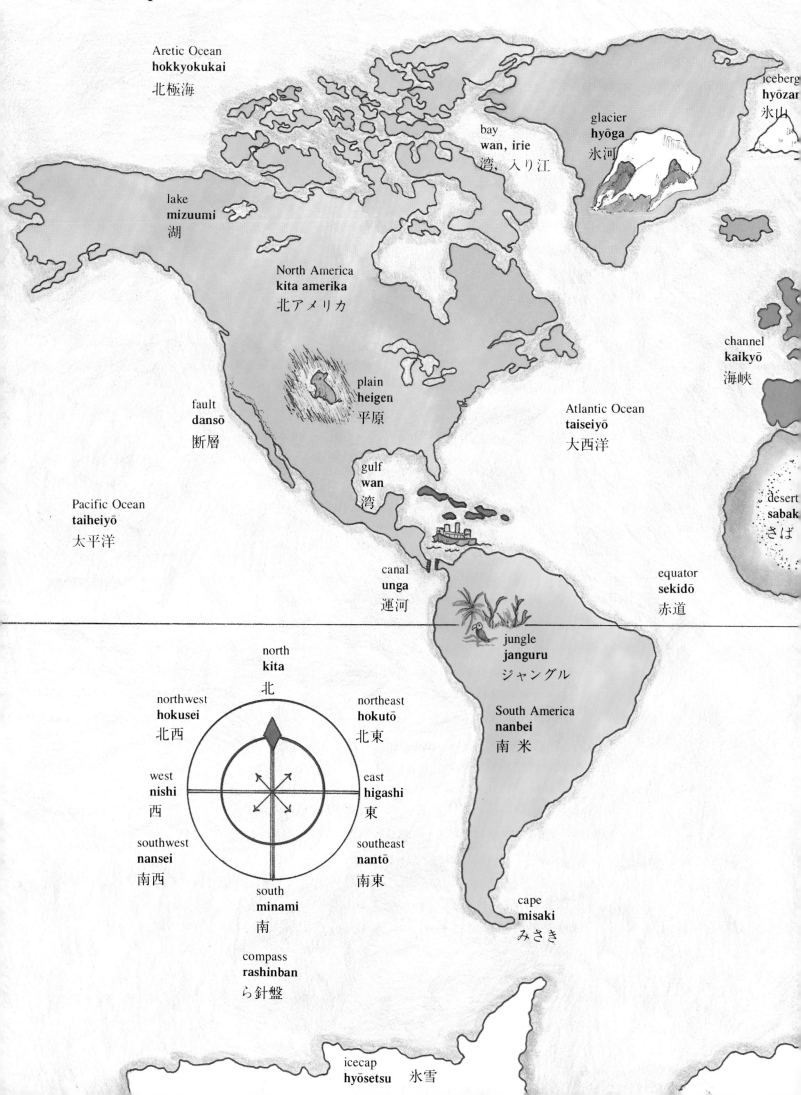

Arctic Ocean
hokkyokukai
北極海

bay
wan, irie
湾, 入り江

glacier
hyōga
氷河

iceberg
hyōzan
氷山

lake
mizuumi
湖

North America
kita amerika
北アメリカ

channel
kaikyō
海峡

plain
heigen
平原

fault
dansō
断層

Atlantic Ocean
taiseiyō
大西洋

gulf
wan
湾

desert
sabaku
さば

Pacific Ocean
taiheiyō
太平洋

canal
unga
運河

equator
sekidō
赤道

jungle
janguru
ジャングル

South America
nanbei
南米

north
kita
北

northwest
hokusei
北西

northeast
hokutō
北東

west
nishi
西

east
higashi
東

southwest
nansei
南西

southeast
nantō
南東

south
minami
南

cape
misaki
みさき

compass
rashinban
ら針盤

icecap
hyōsetsu
氷雪

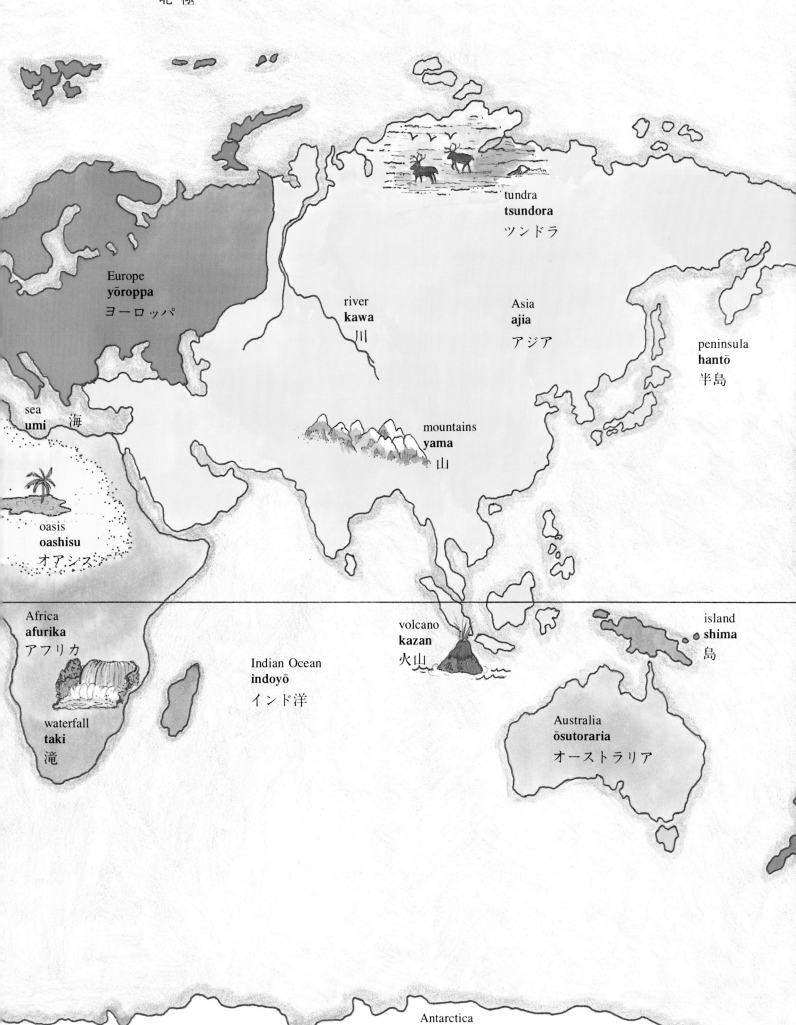

North Pole
hokkyoku
北極

tundra
tsundora
ツンドラ

river
kawa
川

Asia
ajia
アジア

peninsula
hantō
半島

Europe
yōroppa
ヨーロッパ

sea
umi 海

mountains
yama
山

oasis
oashisu
オアシス

Africa
afurika
アフリカ

Indian Ocean
indoyō
インド洋

volcano
kazan
火山

island
shima
島

waterfall
taki
滝

Australia
ōsutoraria
オーストラリア

Antarctica
nankyoku tairiku
南極大陸

South Pole
nankyoku 南極

Japanese-English Glossary and Index

hangā, hanger, 2
hangu guraidā, hang glider, 16
hankachi, handkerchief, 7
hanmokku, hammock, 5
hansen, sailboat, 16
hanshakyō, reflectors, 14
hanten, spots, 20
hantō, peninsula, 32
hanzubon, shorts, 7
hāpu, harp, 19
hari, hand, 1
haru, spring, 5
hasami, scissors, 1, 12
hashi, bridge, 16
hashigo, ladder, 23
hashiri takatobi, high jump, 18
hashiru, run, 27
hata, banner, 25; flags, 17
hatake, field, 24
hayai, fast, 26
hea airon, curling iron, 12
hea dezainā, hairstylist, 12
hea doraiyā, blow dryer, hair dryer, 12
(hea) mūsu, mousse, 12
hea pin, barrette, 12
hea supurē, hair spray, 12
hebi, snake, 20
heddohōn, headset, 17
heddoraito, headlight, 14
heigen, plain, 32
herikoputā, helicopter, 16
herumetto, helmet, 18
hi, fire, 24
hidari no, left, 26
higashi, east, 32
higesoriyō kuriimu, shaving cream, 12
hiji, elbow, 11
hijikake isu, armchair, 2
hijō kaidan, fire escape, 8
hikidashi, drawer, 3
hikōki, airplane, 16, 17
hiku, pull, 27
himo, string, 4, 13
hiraita, open, 26
hire, fin, 22
hiroba, square, 8
hisho, secretary, 15
hitai, forehead, 11
hitobito, people, 15
hitode, starfish, 22
hitsuji, sheep, 9
hiuchi ishi, flint, 24
hiyoko, chick, 9
hiza, knee, 11
hizume, eoof, 20
ho, sail, 16
hō, cheek, 11
hodō, sidewalk, 16
hoeru, roar, 27
hoho, cheek, 11
hohoemi, smile, 11

hoiiru kyappu, hubcap, 14
hojorin, training wheels, 14
hōki, broom, 3
hokkyoku, North Pole, 32
hokkyokukai, Arctic Ocean, 32
hokori, dust, 4
hokusei, northwest, 32
hokutō, northeast, 32
hon, book, 1
hon'ya, bookstore, 8
hon'yasan, bookseller, 15
honbako, bookcase, 1
hone, bone, 24
hora ana, cave, 24
hora ana kaiga, cave drawing, 24
hōrensō, spinach, 6
hori, moat, 25
horu, dig, 27
hōru, auditorium, 19
hōseki, jewel, 22
hōsekibako, treasure chest, 22
hōsekishō, jeweler, 15
hoshi, stars, 23
hoshikusa, hay, 9
hōtai, bandage, 11
hotchikisu, stapler, 1
hotchikisu no hari, staples, 1
hoteru, hotel, 8
hyaku, hundred, 31
hyakuman, million, 31
hyō, leopard, 20
hyōga, glacier, 32
hyōji, sign, 6
hyōsetsu, icecap, 32
hyōshiki, sign, 6
hyōzan, iceberg, 32

ichi, one, 31
ichibanme, first, 31
ichigo, strawberries, 6
ichirinsha, unicycle, 21
ido, well, 24
ie, house, 2
iin, doctor's office, 11
ikari, anchor, 22
ike, pond, 9
ikka no keizu, family tree, 29
iku, go, 27
ima, living room, 2
imōto, sister, 29
inaka, country, 9
inazuma, lightning, 5
indoyō, indian ocean, 32
inu, dog, 9
ippai no, full, 26
ippon sutando, kickstand, 14
irie, bay, 32
iro, colors, 28
(iro ga) koi, dark, 26
(iro ga) usui, light, 26
iroenpitsu, colored pencils, 1
iruka, dolphin, 22
isha, doctor, 11

ishō, costume, 19
ishōire kaban, garment bag, 17
isu, chair, 3
ita, board, 3
ito, string, 4, 13
itoguruma, spinning wheel, 4
itoko, cousin, 29
itoyōji, dental floss, 11
iwa, rock, 24
iyaringu, earring, 7

jagā, jaguar, 20
jagaimo, potatoes, 6
jaguchi, faucet, 3
jakki, jack, 14
jamu, jam, 10
janguru, jungle, 32
janguru jimu, jungle gym, 8
jidō yokin shiharaiki, automatic teller, 13
(jidō) sara araiki, dishwasher, 3
jidōsha, car, 16
jigusō pazuru, jigsaw puzzle, 4
jiipan, jeans, 7
jiipu, jeep, 16
jikkengi, lab coat, 23
jinkō eisei, satellite, 23
jinrui no rekishi, human history, 24
jippā, zipper, 7
jishaku, magnet, 4
jitensha, bicycle, 14, 16, 18
jitensha kyōsō, cycling, 18
jitensha ni noru, ride a bicycle, 27
jō, lock, 13
jōba, horseback riding, 18
jōbu, top, 26
jōgi, ruler, 1
jogingu, jogging, 18
jōkyaku, passenger, 17
jōkyaku gakari, flight attendant, 17
joō, queen, 25
josetsusha (ki), snowplow, 5
joshi ten'in, saleswoman, 16
josū, ordinal numbers, 31
joyū, actress, 19
jōzai, pill, 11
jū, ten, 31
jūbanme, tenth, 31
jūgo, fifteen, 31
jūhachi, eighteen, 31
jūi, veterinarian, 15
jūichi, eleven, 31
jūku, nineteen, 31
jūkyū, nineteen, 31
jūman, hundred thousand, 31
jūnana, seventeen, 31
jūni, twelve, 31
jūoku, billion, 31
jūroku, sixteen, 31
jūryōage, weight lifting, 18
jūsan, thirteen, 31
jūshi, fourteen, 31
jūshichi, seventeen, 31

natsu, summer, 5
nattsu, nuts, 6
nawa, rope, 21
nawabashigo, rope ladder, 21
naya, barn, 9
nebukuro, sleeping bag, 9
nedan, price, 6
neji, screw, 3
nejimawashi, screwdriver, 3
nekki kyū, hot-air balloon, 16
nekkuresu, necklace, 7
neko, cat, 9
nekutai, tie, 7
nemuru, sleep, 27
nendo, clay, 24
nerihamigaki, toothpaste, 11
nēru enameru, nail polish, 12
netto, net, 18
nezumi, mouse, 9, 26; rat, 25
nezumitori, mouse hunt, 26
. . . ni mottomo chikai, next to, 26
ni, two, 31
nibanme, second, 31
nibun no ichi, half, 31
niguruma, cart, 24
niji, rainbow, 5
nijū, twenty, 31
nijū-go, twenty-five, 31
nijū-hachi, twenty-eight, 31
nijū-ichi, twenty-one, 31
nijū-ku, twenty-nine, 31
nijū-kyū, twenty-nine, 31
nijū-nana, twenty-seven, 31
nijū-ni, twenty-two, 31
nijū-roku, twenty-six, 31
nijū-san, twenty-three, 31
nijū-shi, twenty-four, 31
nijū-shichi, twenty-seven, 31
nijū-yon, twenty-four, 31
niku, meat, 6
nikuya, butcher shop, 8
nikuyasan, butcher, 15
nimotsu shitsu, cargo bay, 23
ningyō, doll, 4
ningyō no ie, dollhouse, 4
ninjin, carrots, 6
nishi, west, 32
niwa, yard, 5
nizukuriyō tēpu, packing tape, 13
. . . no aida ni, between, 26
. . . no kahō ni, down, 26
. . . no mae ni, in front of, 26
. . . no shita ni, under, 26
. . . no ue ni, above, on top of, up, 26
. . . no ushiro ni, behind, 26
noboru, climb, 27
nōfu, farmer, 9
nōjō, farm, 9
nokogiri, saw, 3
nomu, drink, 27
nōto, notebook, 1
nuno, cloth, 24
nureta, wet, 26

nurie, coloring book, 4
nyūjōken, tickets, 21
nyūjōken uriba, ticket booth, 21
nyūyoku suru, take a bath, 27

o, tail, 20
ō, king, 25
. . . o sasu, point (at), 27
oashisu, oasis, 32
oba, aunt, 29
obāchan, grandma, 29
ōbun, oven, 3
ōdan hodō, crosswalk, 16
odorite, dancer, 19
odoru, dance, 27
ohajiki, marbles, 4
oji, uncle, 29
ōji, prince, 25
ojiichan, grandpa, 29
ōjo, princess, 25
oka, hill, 9
ōkami, wolf, 20
ōkan, crown, 25
okane, money, 6
okāsan, mom, 29
ōkesutora, orchestra, 19
ōkesutora seki, orchestra pit, 19
ōkina, large, 26
okurimono, gift, 10
omocha, toys, 4
omocha no heitai, toy soldiers, 4
omochaya, toy store, 8
omoi, heavy, 26
ōmu, parrot, 20
omuretsu, omelet, 10
ondori, rooster, 9
onna, woman, 9
onna ten'in, saleswoman, 16
ono, ax, 25
orenji, orange, 6
orenji iro, orange, 28
ori, cage, 21
ōru, oar, 16
oru hito, weaver, 24
orugōru, music box, 4
osagegami, braid, 12
oshieru, teach, 27
oshiire, closet, 2
oshiroi, powder, 12
osoi, slow, 26
osu, push, 27
(osu no) kujaku, peacock, 20
ōsutoraria, Australia, 32
ōtobai, motorcycle, 16
otoko, man, 9
otōsan, dad, 29
otōto, brother, 29
oushi, bull, 9
oyayubi, thumb, 11
oyogu, swim, 27

pai, pie, 6
painappuru, pineapple, 6

pairotto, pilot, 17
pajama, pajamas, 7
pākingu mētā, parking meter, 8
pan, bread, 6
panda, panda, 20
panku shita taiya, flat tire, 14
pan'ya, bakery, 8
parashūto, parachute, 18
pasupōto, passport, 17
patokā, police car, 16
pedaru, pedal, 14
pedikyuashi, pedicurist, 12
pen, pen, 1
penchi, pliers, 14
pengin, penguin, 20
penkiya, painter, 15
pēpā taoru, paper towels, 3
piano, piano, 19
piero, clown, 21
piinatsu, peanuts, 21
pikunikku, picnic, 9
pinku, pink, 28
poketto, pocket, 7
poniitēru, ponytail, 12
poppukōn, popcorn, 21
posutā, poster, 2
pōtā, porter, 17
poteto chippu, potato chips, 6
puropera, propeller, 17
pūru, swimming pool, 18

raberu, label, 13
raimu, lime, 6
raion, lion, 20, 21
raion zukai, lion tamer, 21
rajio, radio, 2
raketto, racket, 18
rakuda, camel, 20
(rakuda no) kobu, hump, 20
ranchi, lunch, 10
rashinban, compass, 32
rēdā sukuriin, radar screen, 17
referii, referee, 18
rei, zero, 31
reitō shokuhin, frozen dinner, 6
reizōko, refrigerator, 3
rejisutā, cash register, 6
rejisutā gakari, cashier, 6
rekishi, history, 24
rekkāsha, tow truck, 14
rekōdo, record, 2
(rekōdo) purēyā, record player, 2
remon, lemon, 6
renchi, wrench, 3
renga, brick, 3
renji, stove, 3
rēnkōto, raincoat, 7
reotādo, leotard, 19
repōtā, reporter, 15
ressha, train, 16
resuringu, wrestling, 18
resutoran, restaurant, 8, 10
retasu, lettuce, 6

tsumekiri, nail clippers, 12
tsumetai, cold, 26
tsumeyasuri, nail file, 12
tsumiki, blocks, 4
tsumugiguruma, spinning wheel, 4
tsuna, tightrope, 21
tsunagi, coveralls, 14
tsunawatari, tightrope walker, 21
tsundora, tundra, 32
tsuno, horns, 9, 20
tsurara, icicle, 5
tsuri, fishing, 24
tsuri hōtai, sling, 11
tsuri ito, fishing line, 22
tsuribari, fishhook, 22
tsurugi, sword, 25

ubaguruma, baby carriage, 16
uchigawa no, inside, 26
uchū, space, 23
uchū fuku, space suit, 23
uchū herumetto, space helmet, 23
uchū hikōshi, astronaut, 23
uchū sutēshon, space station, 23
uchū yūei, space walk, 23
uchūjin, alien, 23
uchūsen, spaceship, 23
ude, arm, 11
udedokei, watch, 7
uēbu no kakatta, wavy, 12
uekiya, gardener, 15
uētoresu, waitress, 10
uetto sūtsu, wet suit, 22
ukeru, catch, 27
uketsuke gakari, receptionist, 13
ukezara, saucer, 10
uma, horse, 9
umagoya, stable, 25
umi, ocean, 22; sea, 32
umigame, sea turtle, 22; turtle, 20
umō, feathers, 20
undōgutsu, gym shoes, 7
unga, canal, 32
uni, sea urchin, 22
unten suru, drive, 27
untenseki, driver's seat, 14
ureshii, happy, 26
uroko, scales, 22
uru, sell, 27

usagi, rabbit, 9
utau, sing, 27
uwagi, coat, 7; jacket, 7
uzumakijō no sokuhatsu, bun, 12

wa, hoop, ring, 21
wagomu, rubber band, 13
waipā, windshield wipers, 14
wakusei, planet, 23
(wakusei no) wa, rings, 23
wan, bay, gulf, 32
wani, alligator, 20
warau, laugh, 27
warui, bad, 26
washi, eagle, 20
watagashi, cotton candy, 21
ya, arrow, 25
yagi, goat, 9
yajiri, arrowhead, 24
yakan, kettle, 3
yakkyoku, drugstore, pharmacy, 8
yakyū, baseball, 18
(yakyūyō) bōru, baseball, 18
yama, mountains, 32
yane, roof, 2
yaneura beya, attic, 4
yaoya, grocery store, 8
yari, lance, 25; spear, 24
yariika, squid, 22
yasai, vegetables, 6
yasashii, easy, 26
yaseta, thin, 26
yasuri, file, 3
yawarakai, soft, 26
yazutsu, quiver, 25
yōfukuya, clothing store, 8; tailor, 15
yoi, good, 26
yoko tonbogaeri, cartwheel, 21
yokuryū, pterodactyl, 24
yokushitsu, bathroom, 2
yomu, read, 27
yon, four, 31
yonbanme, fourth, 31
yonjū, forty, 31
yonjū-go, forty-five, 31
yonjū-hachi, forty-eight, 31
yonjū-ichi, forty-one, 31
yonjū-ku, forty-nine, 31

yonjū-kyū, forty-nine, 31
yonjū-nana, forty-seven, 31
yonjū-ni, forty-two, 31
yonjū-roku, forty-six, 31
yonjū-san, forty-three, 31
yonjū-shi, forty-four, 31
yonjū-shichi, forty-seven, 31
yonjū-yon, forty-four, 31
yoroi kabuto, armor, 25
yōroppa, europe, 32
yoru, night, 21
yōsei, fairy, 25
yotto, sailing, 18
yubi, finger, 11
yubi ningyō, puppet, 4
yubi no tsume, fingernail, 12
yūbin haitatsu kaban, mailbag, 13
yūbin kyokuin, postal worker, 13
yūbin no keshiin, postmark, 13
yūbin posuto, mailbox, 13
yūbin sashiireguchi, mail slot, 13
yūbin shūhainin, letter carrier, 15
yūbinbangō, zip code, 13
yūbinkyoku, post office, 13
yubiwa, ring, 7
yubune, bathtub, 2
yuka, floor, 2
yuki, snow, 5
yuki no tama, snowball, 5
yukidaruma, snowman, 5
yumi, bow, 25
yunihōmu, uniform, 4
yunikōn, unicorn, 25
yūransen, cruise ship, 16
yuri mokuba, rocking horse, 4
yurikago, cradle, 4
yūshoku, dinner, 10
yusō kikan, transportation, 16

zaihō, treasure, 22
zaru, basket, 24
zaseki, seat, 17
zasshi, magazines, 11
zeikanri, customs officer, 17
zenchishi, prepositions, 26
zō, elephant, 20, 21; statue, 8
zubon, pants, 7

English-Japanese Glossary and Index

candle, rōsoku, 10
candy, kyandē, 6
cane, tsue, 11
cannon, taihō, 22
canoe, kanū, 16
cap, kyappu, 7
cape, katamanto, 21; misaki, 32
car, jidōsha, 16
car racing, kā rēsu, 18
car wash, senshajō, 14
caramel apple, ringoame, 21
cardinal numbers, kisū, 31
cards, toranpu, 4
cargo bay, nimotsu shitsu, 23
carpenter, daiku, 15
carpet, jūtan, kāpetto, 2
carrots, ninjin, 6
carry, hakobu, 27
cart, niguruma, 24
cartwheel, yoko tonbogaeri, 21
cash register, rejisutā, 6
cashier, rejisutā gakari, 6
cassette player, kasetto dekki, 2
cassette tape, kasetto tēpu, 2
cast, gipusu, 11
castle, shiro, 25
cat, neko, 9
catch, ukeru, 27
cave, hora ana, 24
cave drawing, hora ana kaiga, 24
cave dwellers, ana kyojin, 24
ceiling, tenjō, 2
celery, serori, 10
cello, chero, 19
cellophane tape, serotēpu, 1
cement mixer, konkuriito mikisā, 16
cereal, kokumotsu shoku, shiiriaru, 6
chain mail, kusari yoroi, 25
chair, isu, 3
chalk, chōku, 1
chalkboard, kokuban, 1
channel, kaikyō, 32
check, kogitte, 13
checkbook, kogittechō, 13
checkers, chekkā, 4
cheek, hoho, 11
cheese, chiizu, 6
cherries, sakuranbo, 6
chess, chesu, 4
chest, mune, 11
chick, hiyoko, 9
chicken, chikin, toriniku, 10
children, kodomo, 19
chimney, entotsu, 2
chin, ago, 11
chocolate, chokorēto, 6
church, kyōkai, 8
circle, en, maru, 30
circus, sākasu, 21
circus parade, sākasu no kaomise
    gyōretsu, 21
city, toshi, 8
clam, hamaguri, 22
clarinet, kurarinetto, 19
classroom, kyōshitsu, 1
claws, tsume, 20
clay, nendo, 24
clean, kirei na, 26
climb, noboru, 27
clock, tokei, 1

close, shimeru, 27
closed, tojita, 26
closet, oshiire, 2
cloth, nuno, 24
clothes dryer, sentakumono no
    kansōki, 3
clothing, mi ni tsukeru mono, 7
clothing store, yōfukuya, 8
clouds, kumo, 5
clown, piero, 21
club, konbō, 24
coat, uwagi, 7
cobweb, kumo no su, 4
coffee, kōhii, 10
coin, kōka, 13
cold, tsumetai, 26
collar, karā, eri, 7
colored pencils, iroenpitsu, 1
coloring book, nurie, 4
colors, iro, 28
colt, kouma, 9
comb, kushi, 12
come, kuru, 27
comet, suisei, 23
comic books, mangabon, 4
community, chiiki, 15
compact disc, shii-dii, 2
compass, konpasu, 1; rashinban, 32
computer programmer, conpyūtā no
    puroguramā, 15
computer, konpyūtā, 23
concorde, konkorudo, 17
conductor, shikisha, 19
cone, ensuikei, 30
constellation, seiza, 23
construction worker, kensetsu
    sagyōin, 15
control panel, seigyo ban, 23
control tower, kansei tō, 17
cook, kokku, 15; ryōri suru, 27
cookies, kukkii, 6
copilot, fuku pairotto, 17
coral, sango, 22
coral reef, sangoshō, 22
corn, tōmorokoshi, 24
corner, kado, magarikado,
    machikado, 8
costume, ishō, 19
cotton candy, watagashi, 21
counter, kauntā, 3
country, inaka, 9
court jester, kyūtei dōkeshi, 25
courtyard, nakaniwa, 25
cousin, itoko, 29
coveralls, tsunagi, kabārōru, 14
cow, meushi, 9
cowboy, kaubōi, 15
cowboy boots, kaubōi būtsu, 4
cowboy hat, kaubōi hatto, 4
crab, kani, 22
crackers, bisuketto, kurakkā, 6
cradle, yurikago, 4
crane, kurēn, 8
crater, kurētā, 23
crayon, kureyon, 1
cream, kuriimu, 10
credit card, kurejitto kādo, 13
crew cut, kakugari, 12
crop, sakumotsu, 24
cross-country skiing, kurosu-kantorii

sukii, 18
crosswalk, ōdan hodō, 16
crown, ōkan, 25
cruise ship, yūransen, 16
crutch, matsubazue, 11
cry, naku, 27
cube, rippōtai, 30
cup, kappu, chawan, 10
curlers, kārā, 12
curling iron, hea airon, 12
curly, kāru shita, 12
curtain, maku, 19
curtains, kāten, 2
customs officer, zeikanri, 17
cut, kiru, 27
cycling, jitensha kyōsō, 18
cylinder, enchū, 30
cymbals, shinbaru, 19

dad, otōsan, 29
dance, odoru, 27
dancer, odorite, 19
dark, (iro ga) koi, 26
dashboard, dasshubōdo, 14
daughter, musume, 29
deck, barukonii, rodai, 5
deer, shika, 20
dental floss, itoyōji, 11
dental hygienist, shika eisei gishi, 11
dentist, haisha, 11
dentist's office, shikaiin, 11
desert, sabaku, 32
desk, tsukue, 1
dice, saikoro, 4
difficult, muzukashii, 26
dig, horu, 27
dining room, dainingu rūmu, 2
dinner, yūshoku, dinā, 10
dinosaur, kyōryū, 24
dirt, gomi, 9
dirty, kitanai, 26
disc jockey, disuku jokkii, 15
dishes, sara, 3
dishwasher, (jidō) sara araiki, 3
dive, tobikomu, 27
diving, tobikomi, 18
dock, funatsukiba, 16
doctor, isha, 11
doctor's office, iin, 11
dog, inu, 9
doll, ningyō, 4
dollhouse, ningyō no ie, 4
dolphin, iruka, 22
donkey, roba, 9
door, doa, 2
door handle, doa no totte, 14
doorman, doaman, 15
down, . . . no kahō ni, 26
down vest, chokki, besuto, 7
downhill skiing, kakkō kyōgi, 18
dragon, ryū, 25
draw, (sen de) e o kaku, 27
drawbridge, hanebashi, 25
drawer, hikidashi, 3
dress, fuku, doresu, 7
dresser, doressā, (kyōdaitsuki)
    keshōdansu, 2
dressing room, gakuya, 19
drill, doriru, 3
drink, nomu, 27

drive, unten suru, 27
drive-in, doraibuin ginkō, 13
driver's seat, untenseki, 14
driveway, shadō, 8
drugstore, yakkyoku, 8
drum, doramu, 19
dry, kawaita, 26
duck, ahiru, 9
duckling, ahiru no ko, 9
dull, kireaji no nibui, 26
dungeon, chikarō, 25
dust, hokori, chiri, 4
dustpan, chiritori, 3

eagle, washi, 20
ear, mimi, 11
earmuffs, mimiate, 7
earring, iyaringu, 7
earth, chikyū, 23
easel, gaka, 1
east, higashi, 32
easy, yasashii, 26
eat, taberu, 27
eggs, tamago, 6
eight, hachi, 31
eighteen, jūhachi, 31
eighth, hachibanme, 31
eighty, hachijū, 31
eighty-eight, hachijū-hachi, 31
eighty-five, hachijū-go, 31
eighty-four, hachijū-shi, hachijū-yon, 31
eighty-nine, hachijū-ku, hachijū-kyū, 31
eighty-one, hachijū-ichi, 31
eighty-seven, hachijū-nana, hachijū-shichi, 31
eighty-six, hachijū-roku, 31
eighty-three, hachijū-san, 31
eighty-two, hachijū-ni, 31
elbow, hiji, 11
electric mixer, mikisā, 3
electric train, denki kikansha, 4
electrical outlet, konsento, 3
electrician, denkikō, 15
elephant, zō, 20, 21
elevator, erebētā, 17
eleven, jūichi, 31
elf, shōyōsei, 25
empty, kara no, 26
engine, enjin, 14, 17
equator, sekidō, 32
eraser, kokubanfuki, 1; keshigomu, 1
escalator, esukarētā, 17
europe, yōroppa, 32
examining table, shinsatsudai, 11
eyebrow, mayu, 11
eyes, me, 11

face, kao, 11
factory, kōba, 8
factory worker, kōin, 15
fairy, yōsei, 25
fall, aki, 5; korobu, 27
family tree, ikka no keizu, 29
fan, sensu, 4, senpūki, 5
far, tōi, 26
farm, nōjō, 9
farmer, nōfu, 9
fashion designer, fasshon dezainā, 15

fast, hayai, 26
fat, futotta, 26
father, chichi, 29
faucet, jaguchi, kokku, 3
fault, dansō, 32
feather, hane, 4
feathers, umō, 20
fence, kakoi, 9
fender, fendā, doroyoke, 14
fern, shida, 24
field, hatake, 24
fifteen, jūgo, 31
fifth, gobanme, 31
fifty, gojū, 31
fifty-eight, gojū-hachi, 31
fifty-five, gojū-go, 31
fifty-four, gojū-shi, gojū-yon, 31
fifty-nine, gojū-ku, gojū-kyū, 31
fifty-one, gojū-ichi, 31
fifty-seven, gojū-nana, gojū-shichi, 31
fifty-six, gojū-roku, 31
fifty-three, gojū-san, 31
fifty-two, gojū-ni, 31
file, yasuri, 3
file cabinet, shorui dana, 13
film, firumu, 21
fin, hire, 22
find, mitsukeru, 27
finger, yubi, 11
fingernail, yubi no tsume, 12
fire, hi, 24
fire engine, shōbōsha, 16
fire escape, hijō kaidan, 8
fire fighter, shōbōshi, 15
fire hydrant, shōkasen, 8
fire station, shōbōsho, 8
fireplace, danro, 2
first, ichibanme, 31
fish, sakana, 1, 10
fisherman, ryōshi, 15
fishhook, tsuribari, 22
fishing, tsuri, gyorō, 24
fishing line, tsuri ito, 22
five, go, 31
fix, shūri suru, 27
flags, hata, 17
flamingo, furamingo, 20
flashbulb, sutorobo, 21
flashlight, kaichū dentō, 3
flat tire, panku shita taiya, 14
flight attendant, jōkyaku gakari, 17
flint, hiuchi ishi, 24
flipper, ashihire, 22
floor, yuka, 2
florist, hanaya, 15
flour, komugiko, 3
flowerbed, kadan, 5
flowers, hana, 5
flute, furūto, 19
fly, hae, 5; tobu, 27
fly swatter, haetataki, 5
fog, kiri, 5
food, shokumotsu, 6
food processor, fūdo purosessā (bannō chōri yōgu), 3
foot, ashi, 11
football, (futtobōru no) bōru, amerikan futtobōru, 18
footprint, ashiato, 23
footstool, sutsūru, 2

forehead, hitai, 11
foreman, genba kantoku, 15
forest, mori, 25
forge, kajiba no ro, 25
fork, fōku, 10
forty, yonjū, 31
forty-eight, yonjū-hachi, 31
forty-five, yonjū-go, 31
forty-four, yonjū-shi, yonjū-yon, 31
forty-nine, yonjū-ku, yonjū-kyū, 31
forty-one, yonjū-ichi, 31
forty-seven, yonjū-nana, yonjū-shichi, 31
forty-six, yonjū-roku, 31
forty-three, yonjū-san, 31
forty-two, yonjū-ni, 31
fountain, funsui, 8
four, yon, shi, 31
four seasons, shiki, 5
fourteen, jūshi, jūyon, 31
fourth, yonbanme, 31
fox, kitsune, 20
freckles, sobakasu, 12
freezer, furiizā, 3
french fries, furenchi poteto, 10
french horn, furenchi horun, 19
frog, kaeru, 9
frozen dinner, reitō shokuhin, 6
fruit, kudamono, 6
fruit juice, furūtsu jūsu, 6
full, ippai no, 26
fur, kegawa, 24

galaxy, gingakei, 23
game, gēmu, gēmuban, 4
garage, garēji, 14
garden hose, mizumaki hōsu, 5
gardener, uekiya, 15
garment bag, ishōire kaban, 17
gas cap, gasorin no futa, 14
gas pump, gasorin ponpu, 14
gas station, gasorin sutando, 14
gate, gēto, 17
giant, kyojin, 25
gift, okurimono, 10
gills, era, 22
giraffe, kirin, 20
girl, shōjo, 9
give, ataeru, 27
glacier, hyōga, 32
glass, koppu, gurasu, 10
glasses, megane, 7
globe, chikyūgi, 1
gloves, tebukuro, 7
glue, setchakuzai, 1
go, iku, 27
go!, susume, 16
goat, yagi, 9
goggles, gōguru, 18
gold, kinka, 22; kin'iro, 28
golf, gorufu, 18
golf club, gorufu kurabu, 18
good, yoi, 26
goose, gachō, 9
gorilla, gorira, 20
gosling, gachō no hina, 9
grandfather, sofu, 29
grandma, obāchan, 29
grandmother, sobo, 29
grandpa, ojiichan, 29

grapefruit, gurēpufurūtsu, 6
grapes, budō, 6
grass, kusa, 9
grasshopper, batta, kirigirisu, 5
gray, haiiro, 28
green, midori, 28
green beans, sayamame, 6
grocery store, yaoya, 8
guitar, gitā, 19
gulf, wan, 32
gym shoes, undōgutsu, 7
gymnastics, taisō, 18

hair, tōhatsu, 12
hair dryer, hea doraiyā, 12
hair spray, hea supurē, 12
hairstylist, hea dezainā, 12
half, nibun no ichi, 31
ham, hamu, 10
hamburger, hanbāgā, 10
hammer, kanazuchi, 3
hammock, hanmokku, 5
hand, hari, 1; te, 11
hand brake, hando burēki, 14
handkerchief, hankachi, 7
handlebars, handoru, 14
handstand, sakadachi, 21
hang glider, hangu guraidā, 16
hangar, kakunōko, 17
hanger, hangā, 2
happy, ureshii, 26
hard, katai, 26
harp, hāpu, 19
hat, bōshi, 4, 7
hay, hoshikusa, 9
head, atama, 11
headlight, heddoraito, 14
headset, heddohōn, 17
headstand, (ryōte to atama o shita ni
   tsukete suru) sakadachi, 21
heavy, omoi, 26
helicopter, herikoputā, 16
helm, kaji, 22
helmet, herumetto, 18
hen, mendori, 9
high jump, hashiri takatobi, 18
hiking boots, haikinguyō kutsu, 7
hill, oka, 9
hippopotamus, kaba, 20
history, rekishi, 24
hockey, aisu hokkē, 18
hole punch, ana akeki, 1
hood, fūdo, 7; bonnetto, 14
hoof, hizume, 20
hoop, wa, 21
horns, tsuno, 9, 20
horse, uma, 9
horse racing, keiba, 18
horseback riding, jōba, 18
horseshoe, teitetsu, 25
hospital, byōin, 8
hot, atsui, 26
hot-air balloon, nekki kyū, 16
hotel, hoteru, 8
house, ie, jūtaku, 2
hubcap, hoiiru kyappu, 14
human history, jinrui no rekishi, 24
hump, (rakuda no) kobu, 20
hundred, hyaku, 31
hundred thousand, jūman, 31

hunter, kariudo, 24
hurdles, shōgai kyōsō, 18
hut, koya, 24
hypodermic needle, chūsha bari, 11

ice, kōri, 5
ice cream, aisu kuriimu, 10
ice cubes, kakugōri, 3
iceberg, hyōzan, 32
icecap, hyōsetsu, 32
icicle, tsurara, 5
in front of, . . . no mae ni, 26
indian ocean, indoyō, 32
ink pad, sutanpudai, 13
insect, konchū, 24
inside, uchigawa no, 26
intersection, kōsaten, 16
iron, airon, 3
ironing board, airondai, 3
island, shima, 32

jack, jakki, 14
jacket, uwagi, 7
jaguar, jagā, 20
jail, keimusho, 8
jam, jamu, 10
jeans, jiipan, 7
jeep, jiipu, 16
jellyfish, kurage, 22
jewel, hōseki, 22
jeweler, hōsekishō, 15
jigsaw puzzle, jigusō pazuru, 4
jogging, jogingu, 18
judge, saibankan, 15
juggle, kyokugei o suru, 27
juggler, kyokugeishi, 21
jump, tobikoeru, 27
jump rope, tobinawa, 4
jungle gym, janguru jimu, 8
jungle, janguru, 32

kangaroo, kangarū, 20
ketchup, kechappu, 10
kettle, yakan, 3
key, kagi, 13
kick, keru, 27
kickstand, ippon sutando, 14
kid, koyagi, 9
kiln, kama, ro, 24
king, ō, 25
kitchen, daidokoro, 2, 3
kite, tako, 5
kitten, koneko, 9
knee, hiza, 11
knife, naifu, 10
knight, kishi, 25
knitting needles, amibari, 4
knot, musubime, 13

lab coat, jikkengi, 23
label, raberu, 13
laboratory, kenkyūshitsu, 23
ladder, hashigo, 23
lake, mizuumi, 32
lamb, kohitsuji, 9
lamp, (denki) sutando, 2
lance, yari, 25
landing capsule, chakuriku kapuseru,
   23
landing gear, chakuriku sōchi, 17

large, ōkina, 26
laugh, warau, 27
laundry, sentakumono, 3
laundry detergent, senzai, 3
lawn mower, shibakariki, 5
lawyer, bengoshi, 15
leaf, ha, 5
leather, kawa, 24
left, hidari no, 26
leg, ashi, 11
lemon, remon, 6
leopard, hyō, 20
leotard, reotādo, 19
letter, tegami, 13
letter carrier, yūbin shūhainin, 15
lettuce, retasu, 6
librarian, shisho, 15
ligh, karui, (iro ga) usui, 26
light bulb, denkyū, 4, 21
light house, tōdai, 16
lightning, inazuma, 5
lime, raimu, 6
lion, raion, 20, 21
lion tamer, raion zukai, 21
lips, kuchibiru, 11
lipstick, kuchibeni, 12
listen (to), kiku, 27
living room, ima, 2
lizard, tokage, 20
lobster, robusutā, 22
lock, jō, 13
log, maruta, 5
long, nagai, 12, 26
long jump, habatobi, 18
look for, sagasu, 27
loom, shokki, 24
loudspeaker, supiikā, 1
luggage compartment, tenimotsu
   dana, 17
lunar rover, getsumensha, 23
lunch, ranchi, chūshoku, 10

magazines, zasshi, 11
magic wand, mahō no tsue, 25
magician, tejinashi, 21
magnet, jishaku, 4
mail slot, yūbin sashiireguchi, 13
mailbag, yūbin haitatsu kaban, 13
mailbox, yūbin posuto, 13
make-believe, maboroshi no, 25
makeup, keshōhin, 19
mammoth, manmosu, 24
man, otoko, 9
mane, tategami, 20
manhole cover, manhōru no futa, 8
manicurist, manikyuashi, 12
map, chizu, 1, 32
marbles, ohajiki, 4
mascara, masukara, 12
mask, masuku, kamen, 19; suichū
   megane, 22
master of ceremonies, shikaisha, 19
matches, matchi, 5
meals, shokuji, 10
meat, niku, 6
mechanic, shūrikō, 14
medal, medaru, 18
medicine, naifukuyaku, 11
medicine cabinet, kusuri todana, 2
medium, chūgurai no, 26

pupil desk, seito no tsukue, 1
puppet, yubi ningyō, 4
puppy, koinu, 9
purple, murasaki iro, 28
purse, handobaggu, 17
push, osu, 27

queen, joō, 25
quiver, yazutsu, 25

rabbit, usagi, 9
race car, kyōsōyō no kuruma, 14
racket, raketto, 18
radar screen, rēdā sukuriin, 17
radio, rajio, 2
rag, borokire, 14
rain, ame, 5
rainbow, niji, 5
raincoat, rēnkōto, 7
raindrop, amadare, 5
rake, kumade, 5
raspberries, kiichigo, 6
rat, nezumi, 25
razor, kamisori, 12
read, yomu, 27
rearview mirror, bakku mirā, 14
receive, morau, 27
receptionist, uketsuke gakari, 13
record, rekōdo, 2
record player, (rekōdo) purēyā, 2
rectangle, chōhōkei, 30
red, akai, 12; aka, 28
referee, referii, 18
reflectors, hanshakyō, 14
refrigerator, reizōko, 3
reins, tazuna, 25
reporter, repōtā, 15
rest rooms, toire, 21
restaurant, resutoran, 8, 10
return address, sashi dashinin jūsho shimei, 13
rhinoceros, sai, 20
rice, gohan, 10
ride a bicycle, jitensha ni noru, 27
right, migi no, 26
ring, yubiwa, 7; wa, 21
ringmaster, engi kantoku, 21
rings, (wakusei no) wa, 23
river, kawa, 32
road, dōro, 9
roar, hoeru, 27
robot, robotto, 23
rock, iwa, 24
rocket, roketto, 23
rocking chair, rokkingu chea, 2, 4
rocking horse, yuri mokuba, 4
roller skates, rōrā sukēto, 16
roof, yane, 2
rooster, ondori, 9
rope, rōpu, 19; nawa, 21
rope ladder, nawabashigo, 21
rowboat, bōto, 16
rubber band, wagomu, 13
rubber stamp, gomuin, 13
rug, shikimono, 1
ruler, jōgi, 1
run, hashiru, 27
running, kyōsō, 18
runway, kassōro, 17

saber-toothed tiger, kenshi tora, 24
sad, kanashii, 26
saddle, kura, 25
safe, kinko, 13
safety deposit box, kashi kinko, 13
safety net, anzen netto, 21
sail, ho, 16
sailboat, hansen, 16
sailing, yotto, 18
sailor, suihei, 15
salad, sarada, 10
salesman, danshi ten'in, 15
saleswoman, onna ten'in, joshi ten'in, 16
salt, shio, 10
sand, sunahama, 22
sandals, sandaru, 7
sandbox, sunaba, 8
sandpaper, kamiyasuri, 3
sandwich, sandoitchi, 10
satellite, jinkō eisei, 23
saucer, ukezara, 10
sausages, sōsēji, 10
saw, nokogiri, 3
saxophone, sakisohon, 19
scale, hakari, 6, 13
scales, uroko, 22
scarf, erimaki, 7
scenery, (butai no) haikei, 19
school, gakkō, 8
school bus, sukūru basu, 16
school (of fish), mure, 22
scientist, kagakusha, 23
scissors, hasami, 1, 12
scooter, kata ashi sukēto, 16
screw, neji, 3
screwdriver, nejimawashi, 3
script, daihon, 19
scuba diver, sukyuba daibā, 22
sea, umi, 32
sea horse, tatsu no otoshigo, 22
sea turtle, umigame, 22
sea urchin, uni, 22
seal, azarashi, 20
seashell, kai, 22
seasons, kisetsu, 5
seat, zaseki, 17
seat belt, shiito beruto, 14
seaweed, kaisō, 22
second, nibanme, 31
secretary, hisho, 15
security camera, bōhan kamera, 13
security guard, keibiin, 13
seesaw, shiisō, 8
sell, uru, 27
seven, nana, shichi, 31
seventeen, jūnana, jūshichi, 31
seventh, nanabanme, shichibanme, 31
seventy, nanajū, shichijū, 31
seventy-eight, nanajū-hachi, shichijū-hachi, 31
seventy-five, nanajū-go, shichijū-go, 31
seventy-four, nanajū-yon, shichijū-yon, 31
seventy-nine, nanajū-ku, shichijū-kyū, 31
seventy-one, nanajū-ichi, shichijū-ichi, 31
seventy-seven, nanajū-nana, shichijū-shichi, 31
seventy-six, nanajū-roku, shichijū-roku, 31
seventy-three, nanajū-san, shichijū-san, 31
seventy-two, nanajū-ni, shichijū-ni, 31
sewing machine, mishin, 19
shadow, kage, 9
shampoo, shanpū, 12
shapes, katachi, 30
shark, same, fuka, 22
sharp, surudoi, 26
shaving cream, higesoriyō kuriimu, 12
sheep, hitsuji, 9
sheet, shiitsu, 2
sheet music, gakufu, 19
shelf, tana, 2
shield, tate, 25
shipwreck, nanpasen, 22
shirt, shatsu, 7
shoelace, kutsuhimo, 7
shoes, kutsu, 7
shopping bag, kaimono bukuro, 6
shopping cart, kaimono guruma, 6
short, mijikai, 12, sei ga hikui, 26
shorts, hanzubon, 7
shoulder, kata, 11
shovel, shaberu, 5
shower, shawā, 2
sidewalk, hodō, 16
sign, hyōshiki, hyōji, 6; kanban, 8
signature, sain, 13
silver, ginka, 22; gin'iro, 28
sing, utau, 27
singer, kashu, 19
sink, (daidokoro no) nagashi, 3
sister, ane, imōto, 29
sit down, suwaru, 27
six, roku, 31
sixteen, jūroku, 31
sixth, rokubanme, 31
sixty, rokujū, 31
sixty-eight, rokujū-hachi, 31
sixty-five, rokujū-go, 31
sixty-four, rokujū-yon, rokujū-shi, 31
sixty-nine, rokujū-ku, rokujū-kyū, 31
sixty-one, rokujū-ichi, 31
sixty-seven, rokujū-nana, rokujū-shichi, 31
sixty-six, rokujū-roku, 31
sixty-three, rokujū-san, 31
sixty-two, rokujū-ni, 31
skate, sukēto o suru, 27
skateboard, sukētobōdo, 16
skates, sukēto gutsu, 18
skating, sukēto, 18
skeleton, kokkaku, 24
ski, sukii o suru, 27
skirt, sukāto, 7
skis, sukii, 18
sky, sora, 9
skydiving, sukaidaibingu, 18
skyscraper, chōkōsō biru, 8
sled, sori, 5
sleep, nemuru, 27
sleeping bag, nebukuro, 9
sleeve, sode, 7
slide, suberidai, 8
sling, tsuri hōtai, 11
slow, osoi, 26

small, chiisai, 26
smile, hohoemi, 11
smoke, kemuri, 9
smokestack, entotsu, 8
snack bar, keishokudō, 17
snake, hebi, 20
sneeze, kushami, 11
snorkel, shunōkeru, 22
snow, yuki, 5
snowball, yuki no tama, 5
snowflake, setsuhen, 5
snowman, yukidaruma, 5
snowmobile, setsujōsha, 5
snowplow, josetsusha (ki), 5
snowstorm, fubuki, 5
soap, sekken, 6
soccer, sakkā, 18
soccer ball, sakkā bōru, 18
socks, sokkusu, 7
sofa, sofā, 2
soft, yawarakai, 26
soft drink, sofuto dorinku, seiryō
 inryō (sui), 10
solar panel, taiyō denchiban, 23
solar system, taiyōkei, 23
somersault, bakuten, 21
son, musuko, 29
soup, sūpu, 10
south, minami, 32
South America, nanbei, 32
South Pole, nankyoku, 32
southeast, nantō, 32
southwest, nansei, 32
space, uchū, 23
space helmet, uchū herumetto, 23
space shuttle, supēsu shatoru, 23
space station, uchū sutēshon, 23
space suit, uchū fuku, 23
space walk, uchū yūei, 23
spaceship, uchūsen, 23
spatula, furaigaeshi, 3
spear, yari, 24
sphere, kyū, tama, 30
spider, kumo, 25
spiderweb, kumo no su, 25
spinach, hōrensō, 6
spinning wheel, itoguruma,
 tsumugiguruma, 4
spokes, supōku, (sharin no) ya, 14
sponge, suponji, 3
spoon, supūn, 10
sports, supōtsu, 18
spotlight, supotto raito, 19
spots, hanten, 20
spring, haru, 5
sprinkler, supurinkurā, 5
square, hiroba, 8; seihōkei, 30
squid, yariika, 22
squire, kishi no jūsha, 25
stable, umagoya, 25
stage, butai, 19
stairs, kaidan, 2
stamp, kitte, 13
stand up, tachiagaru, 27
stapler, hotchikisu, 1
staples, hotchikisu no hari, 1
starfish, hitode, 22
stars, hoshi, 23
statue, zō, 8
steak, sutēki, 10

steering wheel, handoru, 14
stem, kuki, 5
stethoscope, chōshinki, 11
stick, bōkire, 24
stilts, takeuma, 21
stingray, akaei, 22
stirrup, abumi, 25
stop!, tomare, 16
stop sign, teishi no hyōshiki, 16
stove, konro, renji, 3
straight, (chijirete inai) massugu na,
 12
straw, sutorō, 10
strawberries, ichigo, 6
street, tōri, 16
string, himo, ito, 4, 13
strings, gen, 19
stripes, shima, 20
stroller, bebii kā, 16
student, gakusei, seito, 1
submarine, sensuikan, 22
suds, sekken no awa, 12
sugar, satō, 10
suit, sebiro, sūtsu, 7
suitcase, sūtsukēsu, 17
summer, natsu, 5
sun, taiyō, 23
sunglasses, sangurasu, 7
sunroof, sanrūfu, 14
supermarket, sūpāmāketto, 6
swan, hakuchō, 20
sweater, sētā, 7
sweatpants, torēningu pantsu, 7
sweatshirt, torēningu shatsu, 7
swim, oyogu, 27
swimming, suiei, 18
swimming pool, pūru, 18
swings, buranko, 8
sword, tsurugi, 25
swordfish, mekajiki, 22

t-shirt, t-shatsu, 7
table, tēburu, 3
table tennis, takkyū, 18
tablecloth, tēburukurosu, 10
tail, o, 20
tailor, yōfukuya, 15
take a bath, nyūyoku suru, 27
talent show, tarento shō, 19
talk, hanasu, 27
tall, sei no takai, 26
tank truck, tankusha, 14
tape measure, makijaku, 3
taxi, takushii, 16
taxi driver, takushii untenshu, 15
tea, kōcha, 10
teach, oshieru, 27
teacher, sensei, 1
teacher's desk, sensei no tsukue, 1
teddy bear, kuma no nuigurumi, 4
telephone, denwa, 2
television, terebijon, 2
television repairer, terebi shūrikō, 15
teller, kinsen suitō gakari, 13
ten, jū, 31
ten thousand, man, 31
tennis, tenisu, 18
tennis racket, tenisu no raketto, 17
tent, tento, 9
tent pole, tentoyō shichū, 21

tentacle, shokushu, 22
tenth, jūbanme, 31
test tube, shikenkan, 23
thermometer, taionkei, 11
thin, yaseta, 26
think, kangaeru, 27
third, sanbanme, 31
thirteen, jūsan, 31
thirty, sanjū, 31
thirty-eight, sanjū-hachi, 31
thirty-five, sanjū-go, 31
thirty-four, sanjū-yon, sanjū-shi, 31
thirty-nine, sanjū-ku, sanjū-kyu, 31
thirty-one, sanjū-ichi, 31
thirty-seven, sanjū-nana,
 sanjū-shichi, 31
thirty-six, sanjū-roku, 31
thirty-three, sanjū-san, 31
thirty-two, sanjū-ni, 31
thousand, sen, 31
three, san, 31
throne, gyokuza, 25
throw, nageru, 27
thumb, oyayubi, 11
ticket, kippu, 17
ticket agent, kippu toriatsukainin, 17
ticket booth, nyūjōken uriba, 21
ticket counter, chiketto kauntā, 17
tickets, nyūjōken, 21
tie, nekutai, 7
tiger, tora, 20
tiger cub, tora no ko, 20
tightrope, tsuna, 21
tightrope walker, tsunawatari, 21
tights, taitsu, 7
tire, taiya, 14
toast, tōsuto, 10
toaster, tōsutā, 3
toe, ashi no yubi, 11
toenail, ashiyubi no tsume, 12
toilet, toire, 2
toilet paper, toiretto pēpā, 2
tomatoes, tomato, 6
tongue, shita, 11
toolbox, dōgubako, 3
tooth, ha, 11
toothbrush, haburashi, 11
toothpaste, nerihamigaki, 11
top, jōbu, 26
top hat, shiruku hatto, 4
tour guide, tsuā gaido, 15
tow truck, rekkāsha, 14
towel, taoru, 2
tower, tō, 25
toy soldiers, omocha no heitai, 4
toy store, omochaya, 8
toys, omocha, 4
tractor, torakutā, 9
traffic jam, kōtsū jūtai, 8
traffic lights, kōtsū shingōki, 8, 16
train, ressha, 16
train station, (tetsudō no) eki, 8
train tracks, senro, 9
training wheels, hojorin, 14
transportation, yusō kikan, 16
trapeze, buranko, 21
trapeze artist, burankonori, 21
trash, kuzu, 1
tray, bon, torē, 10
treasure, zaihō, 22